Get Off Your Horse!
Fifty-Two Succinct Leadership Lessons from US Presidents

Michael Bret Hood

ISBN: 1548663646
ISBN-13: 978-1548663643
Library of Congress Control Number: 2017912879
LCCN Imprint Name: CreateSpace Independent Publishing Platform, North
Charleston, SC

This book is dedicated to my dad for giving me a love of history as well as all of the people who have shared a leadership course with me. Without you, I would have never had the discussions that sparked many of the ideas contained within.

Contents

Bonus Chapters from Michael Bret Hood's *Eat More Ice Cream: A Succinct Leadership Lesson for Each Week of the Year*

Preface

Get Off Your Horse! Fifty-Two Succinct Leadership Lessons from US Presidents was inspired by you—the reader. Each week, I would share an original leadership articled on LinkedIn in the hopes that the article would spark interesting discussions about modern leadership. I quickly noticed that if I shared an article referencing a story about a past US president, the number of page views increased tenfold. To me, this meant that there was a substantial shared interest in learning about US presidents, their leadership styles, and historical events that helped place their leadership in the proper context.

While it would have been easy to use some of the more well-known historical stories about US presidents, I wanted to dig deeper and gather some of the stories that you wouldn't necessarily recognize. The stories contained within this book's chapters highlight both historical successes and failures. By no means, however, is this book a referendum on any single president's legacy of success or failure. Each US president has made both good and bad decisions, some of which are highlighted within. The presidential stories in this book are meant to be used as a tool to help you reflect on your leadership style by infusing the latest scientific research with certain pivotal moments in US history.

I sincerely hope you have as good a time reading these stories as I had researching and writing them.

Acknowledgments

Thank you to Nancy, Alexandra, Chloe, Harold, Carole, Tonya, Miguel, Radhika, Carl, Tom, Fadi, Jeff, Tony, Dennis, John, Bill, Meredith, Elisa, Latoyia, Jerry, Cory, Beth, Cynthia, Gail, Ken, Russ, Mike, Jeff, Suzanna, Melody, Ed, Damien, and so many others for helping me on this leadership journey.

1. Get Off Your Horse!

Have you ever had a follower come into your office to speak with you and after a few minutes, you find yourself hoping the follower would get to the point so that you could get back to your work? Have you ever glanced over at your computer screen to check your e-mails when a follower is having a conversation with you? Have you ever delegated a task to one of your followers because you felt the task was below your pay level or not worthy of your time? How do these things affect your leadership?

A recent scientific study done by Professor Dacher Keltner has suggested that our brain might have something to do with a leader's inability to do the right thing. People who have suffered head trauma can suffer damage to the frontal lobe, specifically in an area referred to as the empathy network. With the wiring for empathy severed, these subjects become inattentive to the needs of others. What Keltner found in his study is that a person who has power, positional or otherwise, suffers similar effect to the empathy network as the person who has suffered brain trauma.

A gentleman was riding a horse along a trail during a war when he saw three young soldiers trying to move a heavy log off the pathway. A corporal sat on his horse watching the three soldiers struggle to move the log. The gentleman asked the corporal why he was not helping the soldiers. The corporal responded, "I am a corporal. I give orders." The gentleman nodded his head before dismounting. He walked over to the three soldiers, and with the additional set of hands, the four of them were able to move the log off of the pathway. The gentleman got back on his horse and looked over to the corporal and said, "The next time you need help moving a log, call the Commander-In-Chief." With that statement, General George Washington rode off.[1]

Daniel Goleman has postulated the existence of an empathy triad made of cognitive empathy (the ability to understand another person's perspective), emotional empathy (the ability to feel what someone else feels), and empathetic concern (the ability to sense what another person needs from you).[2] How is it that some leaders are able to maintain empathy as they rise in an organization but others lose their ability?

---

[1] S. Aughtmon, "The Heavy Log," *Bay Business Help*, February 15, 2013,
[2] D. Goleman, "The Focused Leader," *Harvard Business Review*, December 2013, accessed July 2, 2016, https://hbr.org/2013/12/the-focused-leader.

The answer may lie in a leader's ability to focus. When you hear the ding from your cell phone, how quick are you to react to the sound? The constant swarm of e-mail, telephone calls, and data has affected leaders. "Not only do our habits of attention make us less effective, but the sheer volume of all those messages leaves us too little time to reflect on what they really mean."[3] Your followers will, at times, struggle with certain tasks at work or with difficulties in their personal lives. As a leader, what does it say to the follower if you do not notice these struggles?

In order to fight against this competition for attention, you have to focus yourself on not only the business at hand but also on the needs of your people. "Where we see ourselves on the social ladder sets the default for how much attention we pay." President Washington always saw himself as an equal to his followers, so when his soldiers needed help, he had no issue with lending a helping hand. In the future, will you even notice if your followers are struggling with something, and if you do, will you get off your horse and help?

---

[3] Ibid.

2. President Lincoln and His Cabinet: How Self-Confidence and Trust Enhance Leadership

One of the hardest things for new leaders to do is to trust not only others but also themselves. If you were to go back in time, how did you lead when you earned your first supervisory position? Did your followers consist of at least a few people who were once your peers? Was the transition to being their leader difficult? If so, was it difficult because of them or because of you?

When we first take new leadership positions, there is an almost innate need to prove we are capable of leading. Yet if we were to self-assess, we'd find that the intent to prove ourselves capable is also about proving that executives made the right decision when they chose us for the position. In our eagerness, we often unknowingly (and sometimes knowingly) push our agenda believing that we are in the best position to know which direction our organization is supposed to go. But is that always true?

In 1860, Abraham Lincoln decided to seek the Republican Party's nomination for president despite three more-prominent rivals, William H. Seward, Salmon P. Chase, and Edward Bates, seeking the same nomination. After Lincoln ended up winning the Republican nomination as well as the presidential election, he appointed all three men to his cabinet, which was heretofore unprecedented. In some ways, these men were better equipped to be president than Lincoln, yet Lincoln had the self-confidence to not only appoint these men but also rely on their counsel.[4]

President Lincoln understood that having capable, well-educated people in his cabinet who were up to date on the critical issues facing the United States would help President Lincoln make better decisions.[5] Instead of forcing his opinion down cabinet members' throats, Lincoln was especially careful in pursuing open dialogue between cabinet members, establishing an open culture where every perspective and idea could freely be challenged by anyone. "Lincoln surrounded himself with people, including his rivals, who had strong egos and high ambitions; who felt free to question his authority; and who were unafraid to argue with him."

---

[4] E. Fried, "An Extraordinary President And His Remarkable Cabinet: Doris Kearns Goodwin Looks At Lincoln's Team of Rivals," *Prologue Magazine* 38, no. 1 (Spring 2006), accessed November 8, 2016, https://www.archives.gov/publications/prologue/2006/spring/intervie w.html.
[5] Ibid.

Some people will theorize that allowing followers to constantly interject and question the leader damages credibility or keeps the leader from making decisions. President Lincoln left no doubt who was in charge, as evidenced by a decision concerning the Emancipation Proclamation. "For months Lincoln let his cabinet debate about if and when slavery should be abolished. Finally though, he made up his mind to issue his historic Emancipation Proclamation to free the slaves. He brought the cabinet together and told them he no longer needed their thoughts on the main issue—but that he would listen to their suggestions about how to best implement his decision and its timing. So even though some members still did not support Lincoln's decision, they felt they'd been heard. And they had been. When one cabinet member suggested that Lincoln wait for a victory on the field to issue the proclamation, Lincoln took his advice."[6] When you allow your followers to play an active role in making important decisions, it doesn't mean that you cede your leadership responsibilities. Rather, listening to different perspectives tells your followers that you realize that you may not always know the best way forward, but more importantly, it sends

---

[6] D. Coutu, "Leadership Lessons From Abraham Lincoln," *Harvard Business Review*, April 2009, accessed November 18, 2017, https://hbr.org/2009/04/leadership-lessons-from-abraham-lincoln.

the message that you fully trust them.

In earlier times, people in positions of power could dictate the direction of the organization from their bully pulpit. Generally, no follower would question the directive unless the leader asked. President Lincoln knew that creating a team of fully competent, experienced, and intelligent people would help him be a better president as well as a better leader. He also understood that to unlock the true potential of his team, he had to go beyond positional power and create an environment where he wasn't the dominant voice until it was time to make the actual decision. "Leaders can no longer trust in power; instead, they rely on the power of trust."[7] By granting trust, listening to the opinions of his cabinet members, and being self-confident, President Lincoln was able to earn the trust as well as the reverence of people who were formerly his primary rivals. Looking at your leadership, how can you expect trust from your followers if you have never first extended trust?

---

[7] C. Green, "Why Trust Is the New Core of Leadership," *Forbes*, April 3, 2012, accessed November 18, 2017, http://www.forbes.com/sites/trustedadvisor/2012/04/03/why-trust-is-the-new-core-of-leadership/#4fcbef805e12.

3. The Father of the Constitution Refuses to Accept the Credit

Is there anything more irritating than someone who takes credit for your work? You've put so much effort into a project or you had a tremendous idea only to have someone else receive the accolades. Is it hard for you to stop the oncoming emotional hijacking? Do you want to interrupt the meeting/proceeding and loudly declare that this was your idea? How badly do you want to expose this person for the fraud he or she is? What if the offending person is your positional leader?

Leaders have an obligation to set the ethical examples for the organization. This requirement extends to middle and lower managers as well due to the fact these individuals are the bridge between the frontline worker and executives. "Good quality relationships built on respect and trust are the most important determinants of organizational success."[8] Yet despite this, there are numerous instances where leaders behave in the opposite manner.

The answer may lie in the acquisition of authority. A number of

---

[8] S. Bello, "Impact of Ethical Leadership on Employee Job Performance," *International Journal of Business and Social Science* 3, no. 11 (2012): 228–36, accessed August 1, 2016, http://ijbssnet.com/journals/Vol_3_No_11_June_2012/25.pdf.

scientific studies have shown that obtaining positional power lessens

empathy for others. "Surveys of organizations have found that the vast

majority of rude and inappropriate behavior, such as the shouting of

profanities, comes from the offices of those with the most authority."[9]

Given these findings, it is not much of a leap for a person to rationalize

why it is suitable to take someone else's idea or work and make it their

own.

While such behavior may help the offender obtain or even

promote in the short term, damage occurs over the long term. In a

study performed by Catalyst, employee engagement increased when

leaders were perceived as humble. "When employees observed

diminished ego in their managers—such as humbleness and

empowering workers—they reported being more innovative and

engaged."[10]

After the United States won the Revolutionary War, the people

---

[9] J. Lehrer, "The Psychology of Power," *Wired*, August 14, 2010, accessed August 1, 2016, http://www.wired.com/2010/08/the-psychology-of-power/.
[10] D. LaBier, "Why Humble, Empathetic Business Leaders Are More Successful," *The Huffington Post*, October 25, 2014, accessed August 1, 2016, http://www.huffingtonpost.in/entry/why-humble-empathic-busin_b_6042196.

were left with the imposing task of how to govern their new country.

The Articles of Confederation were drafted and ratified in 1781. The

document gave most power to the separate states, but leaders quickly

learned that doing so did not allow the federal government to properly

manage debt or sustain a military. Future President James Madison

recognized this and started studying other governmental structures

around the world to see if he could draft a Constitution befitting the

needs of a new republic. In May 1787, delegates from all the states

attended a constitutional convention and Madison unveiled his "Virginia

Plan," which designated three branches of government: executive,

judicial, and legislative. Madison took detailed notes of the discussions

about his plan and used these suggestions to reformulate the

document, which eventually became our Constitution. When referred to

as the "Father of the Constitution," Madison deflected credit by telling

everyone the document was the work of many capable minds. [11]

Although President Madison was essential to creating the

United States Constitution, he preferred to highlight the contributions

of others. Madison understood that he did not and would not have all

---

[11] "James Madison," the History Channel, accessed August 1, 2016,
http://www.history.com/topics/us-presidents/james-madison.

the answers for a growing country faced with new issues every day. By

deflecting credit to others, Madison allowed people to take credit for

what was theirs, which spurred the growth of a fledgling republic. Can

you imagine the growth that could happen in your organization if

people were given credit for their original ideas and work?

4. Stress and Leadership

How do you cope with stress and emotions? Do you face them head on, or do you repress them deep inside your body? No matter how you cope with stress, is it possible that your stress levels have a material effect on your followers? In your estimation as the leader of your group, is that effect positive or negative?

Stress has significant short-term and long-term impacts on your brain as well as your body. University of Iowa researchers focused on short-term stress and found that cortisol, the stress hormone, causes reduced connections in the prefrontal cortex, which is the part of the brain that controls short-term memory.[12] If you can't remember where you placed your car keys, it might be because of short-term stress.

Long-term stress has different effects depending on how the stress originated. In traumatic incidents, for example, stress can increase your ability to encode details from the event. The stress from such an event can endure in your mind, but this type of long-term stress doesn't normally cause damage to your body. If the stress is accumulated over

---

[12] S. Govender and S. Cheshire, "Chronic Stress Can Hurt Your Memory," CNN, June 19, 2014, accessed February 17, 2017, http://edition.cnn.com/2014/06/17/health/memory-stress-link/.

time, however, there can be substantial detrimental effects to both the body and the mind. Chronic stress causes permanent changes in brain wiring, which damages the brain's ability to communicate with itself. This results in an increased chance of experiencing mental illnesses such as schizophrenia, chronic depression, bipolar disorder, obsessive-compulsive disorder, and post-traumatic stress disorder.[13]

According to the Center for Creative Leadership, 88 percent of leaders reported work to be a significant source of stress, and having a leadership role within an organization increased their stress levels.[14] Long-term stress leads to cognitive impairment, which over time can cause your leadership style to change. Leaders who suffer from short and long-term stress are more likely to revert to autocratic styles of leadership as opposed to more effective transformational leadership styles as the brain reacts to the increased pressures. A leader who predominantly leads using the autocratic style will become even more of a dominant micromanager in the presence of both short and long-term stress.

---

[13] Ibid.

[14] M. Campbell, J. Baltes, A. Martin, and K. Meddings, *The Stress of Leadership* (Greensboro, NC: Center for Creative Leadership, 2007), accessed February 17, 2017, http://www.ccl.org/wp-content/uploads/2015/04/StressofLeadership.pdf.

President James Polk suffered from chronic stress, as he would never allow himself to drift away from work. Even when he was away from his office, Polk continually reflected on what needed to be done. President Polk's leadership style was described as "a perfectionist and micro-manager with an obsessive desire to control every aspect of the executive branch." The stress caused by his obsession with perfection affected his leadership style and led President Polk to trust no one. The lack of delegation caused President Polk to place excessive demands upon himself, which in turn, caused him additional stress as he worked even harder to achieve what he felt needed to be done. The short and long-term stress inevitably led President Polk to a tireless circle of taking on more and more tasks to include additional roles such as his sole speechwriter, appointment maker, and chief political strategist all at the expense of his followers.[15]

Leaders who expect perfection from their followers are creating an environment where stress will thrive. If followers feel they are being treated unfairly or given expectations that can't be met, the stress manufactured by the leader means that followers are more likely to

---

[15] P. Brandus, *Under This Roof: The White House and the Presidency—21 Presidents, 21 Rooms, 21 Inside Stories* (Guilford, CT: LP, an imprint of Rowman & Littlefield, 2015).

suffer health issues that could be prevented according to a recent study.

"To some extent, managers and executives may be able to help mitigate

stress-related health issues, and that top down efforts to foster a more

collegial and secure working environment may lead to happier and

healthier workers."[16] Given this research, the way that you cope with

stress has a profound effect not only on you but also on the people you

lead. If this very thought causes you more stress, imagine what it does

to your followers.

---

[16] G. White, "The Alarming Long-Term Consequences of Workplace Stress," *The Atlantic*, February 12, 2015, accessed February 17, 2017, https://www.theatlantic.com/business/archive/2015/02/the-alarming-long-term-consequences-of-workplace-stress/385397/.

5. D-Day: President Eisenhower, Team Building, and Psychological Safety

Have you ever been on a team that succeeded? Have you ever

been on a team that failed? If you can recall, what were the differences

between the two experiences? As a leader, could you take something

from each experience and transfer it to your teams in order to ensure

their success?

Collaboration in the workplace is growing at an unprecedented

pace. Over the last two decades, Harvard researchers have found that

the time spent collaborating in organizations has increased over 50

percent.[17] With so much collaboration, shouldn't there be enough data

to determine why some teams succeed and why some teams fail?

A diverse group of researchers at Google's people analytics

department tried to determine what attributes led teams to success.

Coined Project Aristotle, the Google team spent millions of dollars

studying collaboration and reviewed fifty years of studies, analyses, and

data. They employed top-rated analysts, scientists, psychologists,

---

[17] R. Cross, R. Rebele, and A. Grant, "Collaboration Overload," *Harvard Business Review*, January–February 2016, accessed August 14, 2016, https://hbr.org/2016/01/collaborative-overload.

statisticians, managers, and engineers to find the secret formula for team success. After all of their efforts, Google found no discernible patterns or practices that directly led to a team's success.[18]

Google's money was not wasted, however. There was one thing that became apparent in the data; teams that created a sense of psychological safety, the belief that any team member could offer a contradictory idea without fear of ridicule, were more likely to achieve team success.[19] While you can never accurately predict the subtle differences in human interaction, you, as the leader, can try to create an environment where each team member feels that sense of psychological safety so that they can offer their ideas to the team members without fear of rejection, embarrassment, or ridicule.[20] To build this culture, a leader has to set the tone for others to follow.

President Dwight Eisenhower and the Allies knew they needed a port in Europe where they could land troops, supplies, and equipment. Utah Beach, however, was only a strip of sand, and any troops who

---

[18] P. Woldow, "What Lawyers Can Learn From Google About Collaboration," JD Supra Business Advisor, August 5, 2016, accessed August 14, 2016, http://www.jdsupra.com/legalnews/what-lawyers-can-learn-from-google-49503/.
[19] Ibid.
[20] Ibid.

landed there would need to find a way to move inland before German

reinforcements arrived. A plan was developed for the 82nd and 101st

Airborne units to drop behind enemy lines to help secure the landing

spot at Utah Beach. The plan had been scrutinized many times over by

Eisenhower's team, and despite the number of people who pored over

the information, the substantial risk could not be mitigated. Six days

before the scheduled landing, one of Eisenhower's most trusted

confidantes came forward and indicated that he didn't think the plan

would work.

Years after the D-Day invasion, Eisenhower spoke about his

thought process, and it was clear when he spoke that the decision still

weighed heavily on him. President Eisenhower, to his credit, had

created an environment where his team felt the psychological safety to

offer ideas that opposed what the majority had decided. It took him

four days of deliberation before Eisenhower eventually decided to allow

the order for the 82nd and the 101st Airborne units to stand. President

Eisenhower appreciated the honesty and candidness of British air chief

marshal Sir Trafford Leigh-Mallory who remained a part of Eisenhower's

trusted team after the invasion, even though Leigh-Mallory was proven incorrect in his calculations.[21]

Google has helped us to prove what President Eisenhower and others already knew—good teams depend on members being allowed to openly provide their thoughts and ideas without fear of consequence. Leaders are only as good as the team members who surround them, and any team needs psychological safety to function properly. As a leader, would you rather have your team members tell you what they think you want to hear, or would you rather have them tell you their true thoughts?

---

[21] V. Lauder, "Eisenhower's 'Soul-Racking' D-Day Decision," CNN, June 6, 2014, accessed August 14, 2016, http://edition.cnn.com/2014/06/05/opinion/lauder-eisenhower-d-day-anguish/.

6. President John Quincy Adams and Bounded Ethicality

Do you consider yourself to be an ethical and moral person? Would you be willing to stand for what is right even though it may cause personal harm? What effect does perception have on determining your definition of the right and just action? How would your leadership be affected if you weren't as moral and ethical as you think yourself to be?

When you make a decision involving a conflict of interest, you might believe that you are objectively looking at the information available, giving appropriate weight to each factor. Automaticity, those brain functions that occur outside of conscious awareness, interferes with your judgments, leading you to bounded ethicality, the belief you are making ethical and moral decisions, when in fact you are unknowingly succumbing to a conflict of interest. "The automatic nature of self-interest gives it a primal power to influence judgment and make it difficult for people to understand its influence on their judgment, let alone eradicate its influence."[22] Bounded ethicality blurs your vision

---

[22] D. Moore and G. Loewenstein, "Self-Interest, Automaticity, and the Psychology of Conflict of Interest," *Social Justice Research* 17, no. 2 (2004): 189–202, accessed January 22, 2017,

causing you to place your personal interests over true objectivity, but your followers don't suffer the same blindness and see your actions for what they are.

By all accounts, President John Quincy Adams was a religious person who believed in the basic moral teachings of the Bible. With his father serving as the second US president, John Quincy Adams also felt familial pressures to succeed as his father had done before him. John Quincy Adams appeared to be ready to follow in his father's footsteps when he served as the secretary of state for President James Monroe. At this time in history, the secretary of state position was deemed as the last step before ascending to the presidency.

John Quincy Adams ran for president of the United States in 1824, facing three other candidates to include Andrew Jackson. When the votes were counted, Andrew Jackson finished with 99 electoral votes and 152,101 popular votes, John Quincy Adams finished with 84 electoral votes and 114,023 popular votes, William H. Crawford finished with 41 electoral votes and 46,979 popular votes, and Henry Clay finished with 37 electoral votes and 47,217 popular votes. The lack of

---

https://www.andrew.cmu.edu/user/gl20/GeorgeLoewenstein/Papers_fi
les/pdf/Self-IntAutoPsychConflictInt.pdf.

any candidate receiving a majority of the electoral votes invoked the

Twelfth Amendment, which meant that the House of Representatives

would determine who would become the next US president, choosing

from the three candidates with the highest amount of electoral votes.[23]

Immediately, John Quincy Adams, Andrew Jackson, and William H.

Crawford tried to influence House of Representatives members.

Bargains and behind-the-scene deals were made. Despite Jackson

having more electoral votes and more popular votes than the other

candidates, the House of Representatives selected John Quincy Adams

as the sixth president of the United States. In order to secure the votes

needed to become president, Adams entered into multiple secret

alliances including making the promise to name Clay, who was the

Speaker of the House, his secretary of state. Jackson and others referred

to these promises as the "corrupt bargain." Jackson would use

references to the "corrupt bargain" to win the presidency over

President Adams in the election of 1828.

It is likely that bounded ethicality stunted President John Quincy

---

[23] E. Lengel, "Adams Vs. Jackson: The Election of 1824," The Gilder
Lehrman Institute of American History, 2012, accessed January 22,
2017, https://www.gilderlehrman.org/history-by-era/age-
jackson/essays/adams-v-jackson-election-1824.

28

Adams's ability to properly judge how these "corrupt bargains" would affect his leadership. "Ethical decisions almost always involve consequences for self and/or others, and it is this social component that brings forth a surge of self-oriented motivations in ethical decision-making."[24] His self-interest altered his judgment allowing bounded ethicality to work its magic.

A desire to succeed is nothing for which you should be ashamed. The route you follow to achieve that success is where your leadership will be affected. Since bounded ethicality operates in a subconscious state, you have to make continued commitments to being a neutral and impartial leader. Simple things such as publicly committing to being a fair leader can help you avoid the effects of bounded ethicality. The next time you are faced with an important decision, ask yourself how the decision would affect you and whether your chosen action serves a personal need or helps to better the followers you are supposed to serve.

---

[24] Dolly Chugh, Max H. Bazerman, and Mahzarin R. Banaji, "Bounded Ethicality as a Psychological Barrier to Recognizing Conflicts of Interest," in *Conflicts of Interest*, eds. D. Moore, G. Loewenstein, D. Cain, and M. H. Bazerman (Cambridge: Cambridge University Press, 2005) pp. 78-79.

7. President Clinton's Social Intelligence

Was there a leader in your life who could just sense whether you needed a compliment or a push to get you going? How were they able to figure out what you needed? If you were asked today, could you identify the expectations and motivations of each and every one of your followers? If not, can you categorize yourself as an effective leader?

Social intelligence is defined as a set of interpersonal skill competencies based in neural circuitry that help to inspire others to be effective.[25] Numerous studies have shown that leader's behaviors are contagious, but that phenomenon is further explained by the concept of mirror neurons. "When we consciously or unconsciously detect someone else's emotions through their actions, our mirror neurons reproduce those emotions."[26] Marie Dasborough conducted a study where one set of participants received negative feedback delivered by a person who also exhibited positive signals such as nods and smiles. The other set received positive feedback with negative signals such as frowns and narrowed eyes. The people who received the positive feedback with negative signals reported feeling worse about their

---

[25] D. Goleman and R. Boyatzis, "Social Intelligence and the Biology of Leadership," *Harvard Business Review*, September 2008, 1–9.
[26] Ibid.

evaluation than did the people who received negative feedback with positive signals.[27] As can be expected, leaders who are high in social intelligence tend to vastly outperform leaders who lack the skills to connect with followers.

Your ability to communicate, effectively or ineffectively, has significant effects on the bonds you make with your followers. "Smart leaders today, we have found, engage with employees in a way that resembles an ordinary person-to-person conversation more than it does a series of commands on high."[28] Listening and watching for cues to people's emotional states can increase the connection between leader and follower. "Researchers have found that the leader-follower dynamic is not a case of two (or more) independent brains reacting consciously or unconsciously to each other. Rather, the individual minds become, in a sense, fused into a single system."[29]

President Clinton wasn't always a great communicator nor could he connect with audiences as proficiently as he does today. In 1988, he

---

[27] Ibid.

[28] B. Groysberg and M. Slind, "Leadership Is a Conversation," *Harvard Business Review*, June 2012, 1–10.

[29] Goleman and Boyatzis, "Social Intelligence and the Biology of Leadership," 1–9.

gave a speech at the Democratic National Convention for the

presidential nominee, Michael Dukakis. The speech, which was

supposed to last for fifteen minutes, drug out for over thirty minutes

and got the most rousing applause when Clinton said, "And in

conclusion." President Clinton, however, used that failure to learn and

refine his social-intelligence skills and eventually became recognized as

one of the great speakers in presidential history.[30]

President Clinton was a master at using pauses in delivery to get his

point across. When Clinton got to certain points he wanted to

emphasize, he would slow down his delivery and let each word sink in

for meaning.[31] By doing so, President Clinton varied his cadence, which

not only increases people's propensity to listen but also allows the

content resonate within people's minds, leading to increased retention

rates.

President Clinton also mastered the ability to connect with people.

No matter how big the room or how big the audience, Clinton had a way

---

[30] S. Harrison, "3 Techniques Bill Clinton uses to Wow an Audience," Fast Company, September 6, 2012, accessed March 9, 2017, https://www.fastcompany.com/3001087/3-techniques-bill-clinton-uses-wow-audience.
[31] Ibid.

of reassuring people that he genuinely empathized with them. Eye contact was a Clinton specialty. "He will look at someone in the audience and speak to them as if they were the only two people in the room. After a few seconds, like most people, that audience member may look away feeling uncomfortable with being singled out by the speaker. Yet when they look back they will see President Clinton still looking directly at him or her with an expression that says 'It's OK,' instantly establishing a direct and personal connection."[32]

President Clinton also leverages nonverbal behavior in very powerful ways while communicating with followers. When Clinton speaks, the quiet nods of agreement, the biting of his lip as you share some painful experience, and the squinting of his eyes when he makes statements of determination are all means to convey the powerful message that he has heard your concerns.[33]

Yet the asset that President Clinton possessed that had the most effect on his followers was his ability to focus and listen

---

[32] S. Mainwaring, "The Magic of President Clinton and How You Get It," *Forbes*, November 9, 2012, accessed March 9, 2017, https://www.forbes.com/sites/simonmainwaring/2012/11/09/the-magic-of-president-clinton-and-how-you-get-it/#35d1771026a1.
[33] Harrison, "3 Techniques Bill Clinton Uses to Wow an Audience."

attentively. "As a politician, Clinton understood the difference between talking at people and talking to or with them."[34] When people feel like their leader is fully engaged in their conversation, the mirror neurons fire repeatedly. "Few behaviors enhance conversational intimacy as much as attending to what people say."[35] President Clinton had the ability to make you feel like you were the only person in the room, even though there were thousands of people around you, because he focused and listened, which allowed him to leverage his social-intelligence skills.

If you fail to recognize the verbal and nonverbal signals being transmitted by your followers, how can you expect to utilize social intelligence? Are you capable of focusing and listening enough to decipher the signals being sent? Out of curiosity, how many times have you checked your phone or looked at your inbox while reading this article? Imagine how those actions would impact a conversation with one of your followers.

---

[34] "Bill Clinton Has a Superpower and Mastering It Can Make You Successful Beyond Belief," *Huffington Post*, August 8, 2013, accessed March 14, 2017, http://www.huffingtonpost.com/2013/08/08/bill-clinton_n_3718956.html.
[35] Groysberg and Slind, "Leadership Is a Conversation," 1–10.

8. How Motivated Blindness Scarred President Franklin Roosevelt's Legacy

Have you ever done something really dumb? Did having the benefit of hindsight make you question your decision or action even more? Did you or your followers wonder what you were thinking and how you could have ever moved forward in that instance? The reasons behind your decision or action may be a perfect example of why you are not as good as you think you are when it comes to self-assessing your leadership.

One of the tenets of emotional intelligence is the need for a leader to self-assess. You and other leaders may believe yourself capable of being an objective judge of your abilities, but your brain frequently works on a subconscious level clouding your ability to be objective without you realizing it. Social scientists identified a human behavior referred to as "motivated blindness," which is described as your ability to overlook bad news as well as how you fail to notice unethical behavior when it is in your best interest not to do so.[36] Can you really objectively self-assess when your brain is very aware of exactly what

---

[36] C. Pazzanese, "Seeing What Leaders Miss," Harvard Gazette, August 7, 2014, accessed February 4, 2017, http://news.harvard.edu/gazette/story/2014/08/missed-opportunities/.

you want?

In Executive Order 9066 signed by President Franklin Roosevelt on February 19, 1942, the US military was authorized to remove anyone from any area of the country if it was deemed necessary for national security. This executive order was signed after the Japanese bombed Pearl Harbor and led to the forced relocation of approximately 110,000 Japanese Americans to various internment camps within the United States against their will.[37]

Members of President Roosevelt's cabinet first proffered the idea of mass incarceration of Japanese Americans based on the fear that American citizens with a Japanese heritage would subvert American wartime efforts. However, there were also voices within the same cabinet against the idea of internment.[38] President Roosevelt suspended the due process of Japanese Americans but failed to do the same against Italian Americans and German Americans whose heritage was

---

[37] R. Medoff, "Why Didn't FDR Help European Jews? Hints in His Decision to Intern Japanese-Americans," Tablet, February 4, 2014, accessed February 4, 2017, http://www.tabletmag.com/jewish-news-and-politics/162780/roosevelt-japanese-internment.
[38] Ibid.

also related to the Axis powers.[39]

According to Greg Robinson, author of *By Order of the President*, prior to becoming president, Roosevelt held negative views about Asians in general. "The future president asserted that the mingling of Asiatic blood with American or European blood produces, in nine cases out of ten, the most unfortunate results." In other writings, President Roosevelt also revealed his deeper issues with people of Asian descent. "Because Japanese immigrants are not capable of assimilation into the American population, they could not be trusted."[40]

President Roosevelt is widely considered to be one of the best American Presidents in history, yet the Japanese American internment camps show that even the best of us are subject to misjudging things due to our base interests and beliefs. In this case, President Roosevelt and others, to include the United States Supreme Court and the American Civil Liberties Union, experienced motivated blindness, in that

---

[39] F. Wu, "FDR New Deal Legacy Intact, But Internment of Japanese-Americans Lives in Infamy Too," *US News*, February 19, 2009, accessed February 4, 2017, http://www.usnews.com/opinion/articles/2009/02/19/fdr-new-deal-legacy-intact-but-internment-of-japanese-americans-lives-in-infamy-too.
[40] Medoff, "Why Didn't FDR Help European Jews?"

they failed to see the ethical issues involved due to the fact that the

United States was drawn into a war with Japan after the horrific attack

on December 6, 1941. Motivated blindness is a common affliction for

leaders. "Even leaders who have gained tremendous success through

focus and application in one arena sometimes lack the self-awareness to

routinely question whether information on which they're basing

decisions is reliable."[41]

The key to defeating motivated blindness is first, to recognize that

despite your best efforts, self-interest frequently trumps logic without

you recognizing it. A leader who establishes an open culture where

followers are allowed to offer opinions and question conclusions can

also mitigate the effects of motivated blindness. The next time you

decide to self-assess as a leader, maybe you should find someone who is

motivated to alert you to your blind spots.

---

[41] Pazzanese, "Seeing What Leaders Miss."

9. President Reagan and Leadership: How the Art of Self-Deprecation Can Lead to Improved Connectivity between Leader and Follower

What is the hardest thing for you to do when promoted to a leadership position? According to 91 percent of employees surveyed in an Interact/Harris poll done for the Harvard Business Review, establishing genuine connections between leader and follower is their number one complaint.[42] Knowing followers' concerns, can you articulate what steps you are taking to establish meaningful connections with your followers? Are these steps working and how sure are you of their success? If you conducted an anonymous survey among your followers, how would they rate the connection between leader and follower?

In order to succeed in today's world, followers must not only respect their leaders but also have to trust them. "The difference between an organization that stagnates and one that evolves and innovates often lies with the attitudes of employees and managers

---

[42] L. Solomon, "The Top Complaints from Employees about their Leaders," *Harvard Business Review*, June 24, 2015, accessed December 11, 2016, https://hbr.org/2015/06/the-top-complaints-from-employees-about-their-leaders.

towards top leadership."[43] If followers do not trust their leaders, the negative impact on an organization can be substantial, but trust is not something followers grant so easily. Some reasons for follower's lack of trust in their leaders could involve follower's previous life and organizational experiences, a natural skepticism, and the lack of psychological safety in the workplace. Despite these and other trust issues, some leaders pierce these veils with ease using a variety of techniques to engender trust from even the most suspicious of followers.

On March 30, 1981, President Ronald Reagan was shot outside of the Washington Hilton hotel. He was rushed to a hospital as national news broke the story. Although his injuries were certainly life-threatening, President Reagan never lost his ability to make fun of himself despite the criticality of the situation. When Nancy Reagan arrived at the hospital approximately ten minutes after the shooting, President Reagan greeted her by saying, "Honey, I forgot to duck." When the surgeon prepared President Reagan for the operating table,

---

[43] "How Transformational Leaders Use Self-Deprecating Humor," Ideas for Leaders, 2016, accessed December 9, 2016, https://www.ideasforleaders.com/ideas/how-transformational-leaders-use-self-deprecating-humour.

the president responded, "I hope you're a Republican." Even after he

recovered, President Reagan never lost his self-deprecating sense of

humor. In a speech commemorating Berlin's 750th anniversary,

President Reagan joked about how he didn't get to go to many birthday

parties where the celebrant was older than him. When some festival

balloons popped, President Reagan didn't miss a beat, clearly referring

to the earlier assassination attempt by saying, "Missed me."[44]

President Reagan used self-deprecation as a way to connect and

build bonds with his followers. "People like powerful leaders who make

self-deprecating jokes because it makes them seem modest, accessible,

and human, which minimizes hierarchical differences between leaders

and followers."[45] In support of this idea, researchers at Seattle

University presented undergraduates with three different vignettes

showing how a boss introduced a new program manager. In the first

vignette, the humor was directed at the entire group. In the second

---

[44] M. Devlin, "10 Strange Things U.S. Presidents Have Done," Listverse, June 30, 2014, accessed December 9, 2016, http://listverse.com/2014/06/30/10-strange-things-us-presidents-have-done/.
[45] S. Kapur, "How Self-Deprecating Jokes Can Backfire," Business Insider, November 14, 2013, accessed December 9, 2016, http://www.businessinsider.com/how-self-deprecation-can-backfire-2013-11.

vignette, the humor was directed at the fictitious followers. Finally in the third vignette, the humor was self-deprecating and directed toward the perceived leader. Overwhelmingly, the students chose the third vignette as the most effective. "Self-deprecating humor enhances perceptions of leadership ability because it tends to minimize status distinctions between leaders and followers."[46]

When status and power distance can be minimized, it changes the perceptions of the followers while also providing a psychological safety net for followers allowing for honest feedback and suggestions. "Smart, capable leaders who know their stuff are well respected, but employees like and trust leaders who are not only smart, but can occasionally lean back and laugh at their own mistakes."[47] When followers see the leader recognize his or her own fallibility in humorous ways, follower's motivations start to be transformed from extrinsic (do what the leader says or else) to more intrinsic (I want to do what the leader asks) means, as the leader is perceived to be more human and therefore less reliant on positional power to accomplish tasks.

---

[46] E. Markowitz, "Brilliant Leaders Use This Type of Humor (Hint: Think Woody Allen)," Inc., June, 2013, accessed December 9, 2016, http://www.inc.com/magazine/201306/eric-markowitz/humor-self-deprecation-leaders.html.

[47] Solomon, "The Top Complaints from Employees about Their Leaders."

President Reagan used self-deprecation as a leadership tool, knowing that leadership is primarily about people and their choices of who to follow. When he made fun of himself, President Reagan not only lessened anxiety in the time of a crisis but also sent a message that he was just as human as any of his followers. Acknowledging your mistakes by utilizing humor can help you build a bridge with your follower to make that important and trusting connection. Doing so might mean the difference between you being a transformational leader or a leader who simply relies on the power of the position.

10. President Obama and the Fifty-Fifty Bin Laden Conversation

Think back to a recent conversation you had with one of your followers. Who dictated the terms of the conversation? Was it you or your follower? Secondly, who dominated the conversation? Once again, was it you or your follower? Lastly, how much time did you spend listening as opposed to speaking?

The immediate need to react to changes in the marketplace has led to deeper delegation in the decision-making process, thereby negating the top-down command and control structure that used to be so prominent in organizations. Midlevel and frontline managers are now having more of an effect on organizational culture than ever before. In addition, communication from top executives has evolved from one-sided to a more interactive tone where information flows in both directions and becomes more of a dialogue as opposed to top-down directives.

According to a study done by Boris Groysberg and Michael Slind, leaders who are successful are relying on conversational methods to increase employee engagement. They have developed a model of leadership they call organizational conversation. "Smart leaders today, we have found, engage with employees in a way that resembles an ordinary person-to-person conversation more than it does a series of commands from on high."[48] By talking with employees and not at them, you can change the dynamic of the work experience.

Groysberg and Slind identified four elements of organizational conversation: intimacy (getting close), interactivity (promoting dialogue), inclusion (expanding employees' roles), and intentionality (pursuing an agenda). When you develop intimacy and interactivity according to this model, you gain the trust of your followers by truly listening to your followers while also creating an environment that encourages dialogue where your followers feel free to not only offer their opinions but also respectfully provide truthful comments about your leadership as well as organizational efforts. To truly get inclusion from your followers, you want them to believe they are a direct part of the success or failure of the organization. This will lead your followers to become brand ambassadors, storytellers, and thought leaders. Some of your best ideas will come from followers, but only if they have the confidence or belief that they can offer these ideas without fear of

---

[48] Groysberg and Slind, "Leadership Is a Conversation."

retribution or ridicule. Finally, you will need to pursue intentionality by not only creating or sharing the organizational vision but also allowing your followers a say in how that vision is established.[49]

Just as it was for President Bush, capturing or killing Bin Laden was the number-one priority for President Obama. In 2010, the United States had developed enough intelligence to believe that Bin Laden may have been hiding in a compound located in Abbottabad, Pakistan.[50] As President Obama queried his advisors trying to determine the certainty of Bin Laden's presence at the Abbottabad compound, the estimates ranged from 10 to 95 percent. President Obama quickly determined that the chances of Bin Laden being present were equal to the flip of a coin.[51]

When presented with four options, President Obama asked every one of his advisors who were involved to not only choose one of

---

[49] Ibid.

[50] Unknown Author(s) (2011). How Osama Bin Laden Was Located and Killed, The New York Times, May 2, 2011. Accessed October 8, 2017 http://www.nytimes.com/interactive/2011/05/02/world/asia/abbottab ad-map-of-where-osama-bin-laden-was-killed.html

[51] J. Gans Jr., "'This Is 50-50: Behind Obama's Decision to Kill Bin Laden," The Atlantic, October 10, 2012, accessed September 1, 2016, http://www.theatlantic.com/international/archive/2012/10/this-is-50-50-behind-obamas-decision-to-kill-bin-laden/263449/.

the options but also defend it. There were many risks involved,

including diplomatic ones. "The frustrated and fraying relationship with

Pakistan vexed planning and announcement of Bin Laden's killing."[52]

When it came time to make the decision, President Obama had

established intimacy, interactivity, inclusion, and intentionality with his

followers. By doing so, President Obama made his decision, but even

those who had proposed a different solution felt that not only had their

voices and ideas been considered but also they played an important role

in the decision-making process.

Engaging in meaningful conversations with your followers can

assist you when you need to make difficult decisions. "By talking with

employees rather than simply issuing orders, leaders can retain or

recapture some of the qualities—operational flexibility, high levels of

employee engagement, tight strategic alignment—that enable startups

to outperform better established rivals."[53] Are you a leader who simply

dictates what followers should do, or are you a leader who is engaging

in conversation? Which do you think would be more effective?

---

[52] Ibid.
[53] Groysberg and Slind, "Leadership Is a Conversation."

11. Are You Really a Leader? Emotional Intelligence and Manipulation

As a leader, how many times have you heard someone say emotional intelligence is integral to being an effective leader? Have you ever attended an emotional-intelligence course? Do you think emotional intelligence has helped you become a better leader? Finally, do you think that an emotionally intelligent leader is better for followers than a leader who lacks emotional intelligence?

Emotional intelligence, defined as self-assessment, self-regulation, interpersonal skills, and empathy, has been considered a lynchpin of good leadership since Daniel Goleman's book of the same name debuted in 1995. In Goleman's opinion, a person who does not have emotional intelligence will never become a great leader. "My research, along with other recent studies, clearly shows that emotional intelligence is the sine qua non of leadership. Without it, a person can have the best training in the world, an incisive, analytical mind, and an endless supply of smart ideas, but he still won't be a great leader."[54]

---

[54] A. Ovans, "How Emotional Intelligence Became a Key Leadership Skill," *Harvard Business Review*, April 28, 2015, accessed October 20,

The study of emotional intelligence is still in its infancy stages, but cracks are starting to form in the foundation. Adam Grant, a professor at Penn's Wharton College of Business, believes that cognitive ability (the ability to solve verbal, logical, and mathematical problems) is more important than emotional intelligence. In an effort to determine if he was correct, Grant created a study wherein hundreds of salespeople were given two validated tests to measure emotional intelligence. These same salespeople were also given a test to measure their cognitive ability. After administering the tests, the revenues generated by the participants were measured and cognitive ability proved to be five times more powerful than emotional intelligence in relation to sales.[55]

In addition, recent studies have directly correlated emotional intelligence to negative personality traits. "Last year, a group of Australian psychologists reported a correlation between emotional intelligence and narcissism, raising the possibility that narcissists with high emotional intelligence might use their 'charming, interesting and

---

2016, https://hbr.org/2015/04/how-emotional-intelligence-became-a-key-leadership-skill.

[55] A. Grant, "Emotional Intelligence Is Overrated," LinkedIn, September 30, 2014, accessed October 20, 2016, https://www.linkedin.com/pulse/20140930125543-69244073-emotional-intelligence-is-overrated.

even seductive' qualities for 'malicious purposes,' such as deceiving

others."[56] As with any personality trait, the ability to recognize, control,

and even hide your own emotions is powerful. Combine that trait with

the ability to sense and empathize with the wants and needs of others,

and you could see a lethal combination of skills that could be used for

nefarious purposes. "When you know what others are feeling, you can

tug at their heartstrings and motivate them to act against their own

best interests."[57]

Dred Scott was born into slavery in the state of Virginia. Dr. John

Emerson, eventually purchased Scott and brought Scott and his wife to

Illinois and Wisconsin, both free states, after being transferred in service

of the army. When living in those states, Emerson rented out the Scotts'

services for personal profit, which violated Illinois and Wisconsin laws.

After unsuccessfully trying to buy his emancipation from Emerson's

widow, Scott filed a lawsuit arguing for his freedom by stating that

---

[56] A. Giambrone, "When Emotional Intelligence Goes Wrong," The Atlantic, May 2015, accessed October 20, 2016, http://www.theatlantic.com/magazine/archive/2015/05/when-emotional-intelligence-goes-wrong/389546/.
[57] J. Barison, "Emotional Intelligence Can Be Used for Good and Evil (and That's Exactly Why You Need It)," Inc., March 17, 2016, accessed October 20, 2016, http://www.inc.com/justin-bariso/emotional-intelligence-can-be-used-for-good-or-evil-and-thats-exactly-why-you-ne.html.

residing in free states where slavery was outlawed made him a free

person. With conflicting rulings in the lower and appellate courts, Dred

Scott's case made it all the way to the United States Supreme Court.[58]

There were five justices on the Supreme Court who had ties to

the South, but they got word to President James Buchanan that they

would let the lower court ruling stand because they did not want to

make new federal law. However, President Buchanan learned that the

five Southern Supreme Court judges would rule differently on the

matter if a Northern judge would side with them. [59]

Using his emotional-intelligence ability, President Buchanan

took the extraordinary step to personally write Justice Robert Cooper

Grier about this decision. Eventually, President Buchanan persuaded

Grier to side with the Southern judges and rule that Scott and other

slaves were not citizens and therefore, did not have legal standing to

sue in federal court. This ruling also negated the Missouri Compromise

by declaring slaves were property and not people. President Buchanan

[58] "James Buchanan and the Dred Scott Case," POTUS Geeks, March 24, 2012, accessed March 25, 2017, http://potus-geeks.livejournal.com/207197.html.
[59] L. Schwartz, "The Six Most Evil Presidents in U.S. History," Alternet, March 22, 2015, accessed September 22, 2016, www.alternet.org,/culture/six-most-evil-presidents-us-history.

believed that a Supreme Court decision agreed to by both Northern and

Southern judges would put an end to the political debate and cause all

Americans to put the slavery issue behind them.[60] Inevitably,

Buchanan's behind-the-scene actions played a significant role in the

initiation of the American Civil War.

The ability to understand others is an essential part of leadership.

Leaders with high emotional intelligence may, in fact, be better suited

to lead, but there is no guarantee that someone with high emotional

intelligence will utilize those skills for the betterment of others. As with

many things, the ethical makeup of a leader has much to do with how

such skills are utilized. The next time you are practicing emotional

intelligence by gauging a follower's needs and wants, ask yourself if the

decision you make will help you more than the follower. If the answer is

yes, can you really call yourself a leader?

---

[60] "James Buchanan and the Dred Scott Case."

12. President Lincoln and the Power of Stories

If you were asked to recall a scene from one of your favorite television shows or one of your favorite movies, could you do it? Chances are that not only could you recall the scene but you also could recite ample amounts of other insignificant information about the show. If our brain allows us to recall such trivial concerns, then why is it that we forget any number of important details in our regular lives?

Believe it or not, the answer to the dilemma lies in the above narrative. Providing directions, reciting law, or delegating tasks do little to activate followers' brains. However, if a leader turns the message into a story, learning and memory functions change. Understanding and memory are intertwined, so we should not be surprised that the art of storytelling increases our probability of remembering.[61] Still, telling a story, especially one that lacks emotion and interesting details, is not enough to ensure it will be encased in someone's long-term memory.

Memories are encoded in a part of the brain called the cortex. During this process, the cortex communicates with the hippocampus,

---

[61] E. Cooke, "How Narratives Can Aid Memory," *The Guardian*, January 15, 2012, accessed August 1, 2016, https://www.theguardian.com/lifeandstyle/2012/jan/15/story-lines-facts.

which analyzes the information and compares it to other stored

memories.[62] If the information is deemed necessary to store in long-

term memory, a memory-consolidation process starts, where the

memory is stabilized after acquisition.[63] Stories help solidify the memory

consolidation.

In addition, leaders can use stories to influence others. Uri Hasson,

a researcher from Princeton University, found that stories could get

people to think like you. "When we tell stories to others that have

helped us shape our thinking and our way of life, we can have the same

effect on them too."[64] Leaders can illustrate important details or actions

through the use of stories to increase retention as well as adoption.

President Abraham Lincoln was known as a master storyteller.

Lincoln had an entire catalog of stories in his head that he could recall

with great detail and explicit timing. While President Lincoln certainly

told stories for pure enjoyment as well as to relieve the sadness within

[62] "Memory Encoding," human-memory.net, accessed August 1, 2016,
http://www.human-memory.net/processes_encoding.html.
[63] "Memory Consolidation," human-memory.net, accessed August 1,
2016, http://www.human-memory.net/processes_consolidation.html.
[64] L. Widrich, "The Science of Storytelling: What Listening to a Story
Does to Our Brains," *Buffer Social*, November 29, 2012, accessed August
1, 2016, https://blog.bufferapp.com/science-of-storytelling-why-telling-
a-story-is-the-most-powerful-way-to-activate-our-brains.

his psyche, he also understood the importance of stories as a metaphor for learning and influencing. "Lincoln could find a story 'to explain a meaning or enforce a point, the aptness which was always perfect.'"[65] Lincoln used his storytelling prowess to illustrate points, help people overcome emotional hijackings, and assist others in figuring out what they needed to do. By allowing others to take ownership of the idea through the relation of their crisis to the moral of the story, Lincoln influenced in ways people did not always recognize.

Communication between leaders and followers is frequently listed as a major issue in organizational surveys. It is certainly easier to provide an order or give explicit directions to a follower when something needs to be accomplished. However, that may not be the most effective way to increase retention or improve performance. Our brains are wired in such a way that the more emotional and the more colorful our descriptions are, the more our brains are activated. Leaders do not necessarily have to memorize a catalog of stories like President Lincoln did. But, if we can find a corresponding memory or event to

---

[65] "Abraham Lincoln's Stories and Humor," the Lehrman Institute, accessed August 1, 2016, http://www.abrahamlincolnsclassroom.org/abraham-lincoln-in-depth/abraham-lincolns-stories-and-humor/.

illustrate our point, our followers might remember or do exactly what we need.

13. Why Experience Isn't Always the Answer

How much do you rely upon your past experiences when leading? Whether the experience is good or bad, do you think recalling the experience will guide you through whatever dilemma you are facing? Does the recall of previous memories help you or hurt you when making decisions? Lastly, is there a chance that your brain can unconsciously lead you to a certain decision without you realizing it?

Whenever we face a decision, a new experience, or a difficult dilemma, our brains automatically search through our memories. "Faced with a new situation, we make assumptions based on prior experiences and judgments."[66] Inasmuch as our brains naturally do not like uncertainty, we often take our existing experiences and make them fit into a situation we are facing, even though the facts of the current situation may not match the facts in our experienced situation. By developing patterns based on past experiences, you try to avoid the stress of the unknown. "Our brains are geniuses at patterned recognition. We collect all sorts of data and we create a pattern. And

---

[66] A. Campbell, J. Whitehead, and S. Finkelstein, "Why Good Leaders Make Bad Decisions," *Harvard Business Review*, February 2009, accessed May 15, 2017, https://hbr.org/2009/02/why-good-leaders-make-bad-decisions.

whether or not we act on that pattern depends on our emotions."[67]

This contradiction can lead us to believe we, as leaders, have the answer, but our solution may have inherent faults. "Most people will think, of course, experience is a good thing. And in many instances, it is. But the reality is that if that experience is not closely tailored with the situation that you're in, it could lead you astray. It could lead you in the wrong direction."[68] If a leader sets his or her default to rely on previous experience without considering the uniqueness of that experience, that same leader is increasing the potential for failure.

In 1989 and 1990, the United States, under the direction of President George H. W. Bush, was trying to persuade Iraq and Saddam Hussein into joining a coalition against Iran. Iraq had previously fought an eight-year war against Iran. Despite intelligence showing a military buildup by Iraq on the Kuwaiti border, President Bush and others believed, based on their experiences, that Iraq would not pursue an invasion. "The premise that the best way to handle Mr. Hussein and

[67] S. Green, "Why Smart People Make Bad Decisions," *Harvard Business Review*, February 2009, accessed May 15, 2017, https://hbr.org/2009/02/why-smart-people-make-bad-deci.html.
[68] S. Green, "Why Smart People Make Bad Decisions," *Harvard Business Review*, February, 2009, accessed October 27, 2016, https://hbr.org/2009/02/why-smart-people-make-bad-deci.html.

moderate his behavior was through improving relations with Baghdad.

That assessment presumed that Iran and Iraq, both exhausted by their

eight-year border war, would focus on domestic reconstruction, not

foreign adventurism."[69]

However, communication involves two parties, and what one

person intends to say is not what one person eventually hears. US

ambassador April Glaspie had a meeting with Saddam Hussein eight

days before the Kuwaiti invasion. In this meeting, Glaspie urged Hussein

to peacefully pursue any differences with Kuwait officials, but then she

also added, "We have no opinion on the Arab-Arab conflicts, like your

border disagreement with Kuwait."[70] Iraqi President Saddam Hussein

could have taken this statement as an indication that the United States

would not intervene if Iraqi forces invaded Kuwait. On August 2, 1990,

Iraq invaded Kuwait.

Experience can be a valuable asset to a leader, but you also can't

---

[69] E. Sciolino and M. Gordon, "Confrontation in the Gulf; U.S. Gave Iraq Little Reason not to Mount Kuwait Assault," New York Times, September 23, 1990, accessed November 1, 2016, http://www.nytimes.com/1990/09/23/world/confrontation-in-the-gulf-us-gave-iraq-little-reason-not-to-mount-kuwait-assault.html?pagewanted=all.
[70] Ibid.

discount emotion in the decision-making process. "Decision-making is not a rational, step-by-step process. It doesn't follow the textbook that says let's identify a set of alternatives."[71] You may believe that the decision-making process involves you weighing the costs versus the benefits of any situation before making the proper choice. Your brain, however, works silently in the background injecting emotion into your decision-making process without you realizing it. Most of the time, your experience will prove invaluable when leading. However, there will be times where emotion will drive your decision, but your brain will tell you that experience led you to the decision. In those moments where emotion trumps experience, will you be able to recognize the need to step back in order to lead effectively?

[71] Green, "Why Smart People Make Bad Decisions."

14. President Warren Harding's "Tone at the Top"

"Tone at the top" is frequently referred to as executive

management's outlook on ethical and moral behavior. In your career,

have you ever been involved in an organization where a leader lacked

accountability? What were the effects of the leader's actions on the

organizational culture? Did you and others enjoy working for this leader

or the organization? Did the leader's lack of accountability transfer to

the behavior of other organizational members?

How many times have you seen someone yawn only to find

yourself yawning a few seconds later. We copy the behavior as a form of

empathy and to increase the social bonds with each other.

Unfortunately, bad behavior, especially on the part of organizational

leaders, can also be mimicked. "The more senior the toxic leader in the

organization's hierarchy, the more likely subordinates are to follow suit

and behave in similar ways."[72]

President Warren Harding is almost universally known as the

worst American President ever. With a promise to return the United

[72] L. Bolton and M. Grawitch, "When Good Organizations Go Bad: How Organizations May Be Facilitating Workplace Deviance," St. Louis University, March 2011, accessed August 1, 2016, http://www.slu.edu/Documents/professional_studies/OHI-CWB.pdf.

States to normalcy, Harding established a new record by winning more than 60 percent of the popular vote. Harding's version of normalcy quickly became suspect as evidenced by his and his cabinet's actions. Harding was a known poker player and unafraid of making risky bets. While in office, Harding engaged in a game of poker and willingly bet White House china, which dated back to the President Benjamin Harrison era. He subsequently lost the hand and the china.[73]

Losing the White House china may have been bad enough, but what kind of message was sent to other members of Harding's cabinet as well as to all Americans? The evidence was revealed after Harding's sudden death in 1923. In what became known as the Teapot Dome scandal, Secretary of the Interior Albert Fall was charged and convicted of bribery in relation to renting public lands to oil companies in exchange for gifts and personal loans. Other officials involved with Harding at the White House allegedly also took bribes, and Harding himself was accused of extramarital affairs while in office and of drinking alcohol at the White House, a direct violation of prohibition

---

[73] "Warren G. Harding," *Independent*, January 19, 2009, accessed August 1, 2016, http://www.independent.co.uk/news/presidents/warren-g-harding-1417416.html.

laws in effect at the time.[74]

When a leader pays no attention to rules and procedures, followers will act in similar ways. "Senior leaders ultimately set the foundation upon which all subsequent norms and values are built."[75] When Harding gambled away White House china and imbibed alcohol despite the prohibition laws, he sent a message to his staff: laws do not matter. "If a senior leader is known for taking corporate materials home for personal use (i.e., theft) or cutting corners in one's work (i.e., production deviance), others within the organization will likely recognize these behaviors and encode them as appropriate."[76]

President Harding was the ultimate role model for the citizenry of the United States and in some cases the entire world. If he had modeled positive behaviors and followed appropriate rules and procedures, informal pressures associated with group dynamics would have demanded compliance. Instead, President Harding, who admittedly was over his head in the position of president, chose to follow the mantra of

---

[74] "Warren G. Harding," History Channel, accessed August 1, 2016, http://www.history.com/topics/us-presidents/warren-g-harding.
[75] Bolton and Grawitch, "When Good Organizations Go Bad."
[76] Ibid.

"Do as I say and not as I do." Leaders who choose this path should not be surprised when followers ignore the proposition just as easily as the leader has shown.

15. Anger and Learned Helplessness: A Leadership Weapon?

Have you ever been so frustrated as a leader that you threw a real

temper tantrum? Have you ever lost control in front of your followers?

How did you feel when you calmed down? What effect did losing

control have on your followers?

Recently, there have been proponents of a leadership style

where leaders motivate their followers by throwing expansive temper

tantrums. Examples of leaders who have allegedly been successful using

temper tantrums as a motivational tool are Amazon's Jeff Bezos, Apple's

Steve Jobs, Microsoft's Bill Gates, and Oracle's Larry Ellison. Without

these tantrums, some experts would argue that success would never

have come. "When handled appropriately, this style can even be

beneficial to employees and the company as a whole."[77]

A leader who has public temper tantrums also takes invariable risks

with his or her followers. Paul Allen, who was a high-school friend of

Gates and was an original founder of Microsoft, spoke of why he left

---

[77] J. Kendall, "The Temper Tantrum: The Key to Smart Management?," *Fortune*, November 22, 2013, accessed March 6, 2017, http://fortune.com/2013/11/22/the-temper-tantrum-the-key-to-smart-management/.

Microsoft after only six years. "In resigning, Gates' friend of fifteen years explained that he could 'no longer tolerate the brow-beating or tirades' noting that 'the verbal attacks you use have cost many hundreds of hours of lost productivity in my case.'"[78] When you create a culture of fear, some followers may abandon ship. Others, however, may thrive in such a world. Walter Isaacson wrote in his biography of Steve Jobs that some people excelled and were spurred to greater achievements by Jobs's legendary meltdowns. "People who were not crushed ended up being stronger. They did better work, out of both fear and an eagerness to please."[79]

Yet there is an inverse to those who grow stronger under such leadership, and this condition can be referred to as "learned helplessness." Martin Seligman and Donald Hirohito created an experiment where two groups of people were placed in a room with a very annoying noise and an additional group was placed in a room with no noise. In the two groups that heard the noise, one set of group members was able to turn the noise off by pressing a button. The other group could not turn off the noise no matter how hard they tried. The

[78] Ibid.
[79] Ibid.

next day, all three groups' members were placed in a room with a similarly loud annoying noise, which they could turn off if they moved their hand about twelve inches. The group members who sat in the room with no noise the previous day as well as the group members who heard the noise the previous day but were able to press a button to turn the noise off quickly figured out what they had to do to make the room silent. Interestingly, the group members who were forced to sit through the annoying noise the previous day did nothing to try and stop the noise. They sat there motionless and endured the unpleasantness. "In phase one they failed, realized they had no control, and became passive. In phase two, expecting more failure, they don't even try to escape."[80] A leader who continually throws temper tantrums can lead his or her followers into a state of "learned helplessness."

President Lyndon B. Johnson and President Richard Nixon had tempers that were described as volcanic. Chester Cooper was a National Security advisor for President Johnson who often fell victim to Johnson's oversized and overbearing personality. Cooper used to fantasize about standing up to Johnson and saw his chance when President Johnson

---

[80] M. Seligman, "Building Resilience," *Harvard Business Review*, April 2011, accessed March 7, 2017, https://hbr.org/2011/04/building-resilience.

sought his concurrence on an issue involving Vietnam. However, when it came time for Cooper to speak, the words that floated out of his mouth were, "Yes, Mr. President. I agree."[81] Power and force of personality can lead people to agree with your decisions even when they don't.

Nixon was equally vitriolic. When President Nixon's secret oval office tapes were released, the public was allowed to peek through a window in which they had never previously had access. President Nixon frequently alternated insults between different segments of society, feeling comfortable enough to go on many racist and homophobic diatribes.[82]

President Barack Obama also was known to have a temper, but at least on some occasions, it may have worked to motivate people. "The president called Axelrod a 'mother_____r' and stalked out of a meeting after his strategist criticized the president's debating

---

[81] F. Greenstein, *The Presidential Difference: Leadership Style from FDR to George W. Bush*, 2nd ed. (Princeton, NJ: Princeton University Press, 2004), 217–23.
[82] K. Baker, "The Temper Thing," *American Heritage* 51, no. 3 (2000), accessed March 7, 2015, http://www.americanheritage.com/content/temper-thing.

techniques."[83] David Axelrod was the chief strategist for President

Obama and had been instrumental in getting Obama elected first to the

Senate, and then later the presidency. While Axelrod admitted he was

surprised by President Obama's temper tantrum, he deflected the

verbal attack by rationalizing what the president had said. "Axelrod

suggested Obama's irritation with him was actually the president's

frustrations with his own poor preparation for the debate."[84] Axelrod

continued working with President Obama who was able to recover and

significantly improve his performance in the second debate.[85]

If you engage in angry temper tantrums when things go wrong, you

are risking a significant portion of your leadership credibility. Even those

who support temper tantrums as a tool for leadership understand the

limitations. "An excessive reliance on the temper tantrum can create a

toxic workplace."[86] When you are leading, you are going to have to

---

[83] K. Walsh, "Axelrod Reveals a Prickly, Emotional Obama," *US News and World Report*, February 17, 2015, accessed March 7, 2017, https://www.usnews.com/news/blogs/ken-walshs-washington/2015/02/17/axelrod-reveals-a-prickly-emotional-obama.

[84] C. Campbell, "Top Obama Adviser Reveals What Happens When The President Loses His Temper," Business Insider UK, February 17, 2015, accessed March 7, 2017, http://uk.businessinsider.com/axelrod-this-is-what-happens-when-obama-loses-his-temper-2015-2?r=US&IR=T.

[85] Walsh, "Axelrod Reveals a Prickly, Emotional Obama."

[86] Kendall, "The Temper Tantrum."

decide whether throwing a temper tantrum will motivate or alienate

your followers.

16. Was President Washington a Leadership Imposter?

In the quietest of times when you allow yourself to reflect on your leadership journey, do you sometimes wonder if you are truly worthy of leading others? If you are just starting your career, do you ever have a lingering doubt about your ability to lead in the future? Are you sometimes afraid that eventually people will wake up and see you for the real person you are and not the leader they perceive you to be? If you have ever experienced feelings such as this, don't worry. You are not alone.

Many people fall victim to the phenomenon known as the imposter syndrome—the feeling that your achievements, position, or leadership is undeserved and that it is only a matter of time before the people around you find out that you are deceiving them.[87] Oberlin college colleagues Pauline Clance and Suzanne Imes coined the term "imposter syndrome" in 1978 after interviewing women who attributed all of their success to luck. Even worse, these women were afraid that they would eventually be kicked out of school or their position once superiors found

---

[87] B. Kerr, "Why 70% of Millennials Have Impostor Syndrome," The Hustle, November 20, 2015, accessed January 28, 2017, http://thehustle.co/why-70-percent-of-millennials-have-impostor-syndrome?_sm_au_=i5V14fNqJwDjVPt6.

out that they were just fortunate instead of qualified. "Despite strong

track records, these women felt that they didn't deserve their

success."[88] Clance and Imes initially believed that only females suffered

this affliction, but subsequent studies have shown that the imposter

syndrome equally affects both males and females.[89] No matter your sex,

the consequences of imposter syndrome are real, often leading to

increased stress, anxiety, and depression.[90]

There have been a number of notable people who have suffered

imposter syndrome, but one apparent victim who may surprise you is

America's first president, George Washington. While President

Washington was very comfortable serving as the Continental Army's

commander in chief, the thought of being the president of the United

States caused him great anxiety. When the secretary of Congress,

Charles Thomson, was dispatched to notify George Washington that he

was unanimously selected to be the first president of the United States,

---

[88] L. V. Anderson, "Feeling Like an Impostor Is not a Syndrome," Slate, April 12, 2016, accessed January 28, 2017, http://www.slate.com/blogs/browbeat/2017/01/27/all_the_dog_death s_in_the_horror_movie_a_dog_s_purpose.html.
[89] Ibid.
[90] C. Carter, "Why So Many Millennials Experience Impostor Syndrome," Forbes, November 1, 2016, accessed January 28, 2017, http://www.forbes.com/sites/christinecarter/2016/11/01/why-so-many-millennials-experience-impostor-syndrome/#2a6d70e53d40.

Washington responded like someone who suffered from the imposter syndrome. "While I realize the arduous nature of the task which is conferred on me and feel my inability to perform it, I wish there may not be reason for regretting the choice. All I can promise is only that which will be accomplished by an honest zeal."[91]

As Washington traveled to New York to be administered the presidential oath, he had hoped to travel quietly, but the citizenry was not going to allow that to happen. With each town visited, people came to see the new leader of the country. Seeing people with such high expectations was extremely stressful for Washington. The extreme adulation of his countrymen only caused Washington's self-doubt to grow. In Trenton after being met by another throng of jubilant supporters, Washington said, "I greatly apprehend that my countrymen will expect too much from me. I fear, if the issue of public measures does not correspond with their sanguine expectations, they will turn the extravagant...praises which they are heaping upon me at this moment

---

[91] R. Chernow, "George Washington: The Reluctant President," *Smithsonian Magazine*, February 2011, accessed January 28, 2017, http://www.smithsonianmag.com/history/george-washington-the-reluctant-president-49492/.

into equally extravagant...censures."[92]

The procession to New York and the pending assumption of the presidency was almost too much for Washington. In his inauguration speech, his delivery was choppy and his hands were visibly trembling. Long known for his physical grace, President Washington seemed clumsy in his initial address to the people. Even in his speech, he showed signs of suffering from the imposter syndrome. "In the first line of his inaugural address, Washington expressed anxiety about his fitness for the presidency saying that, 'no event could have filled him with greater anxieties' than the news brought to him by Charles Thomson. He had grown despondent, he said candidly, as he considered his own 'inferior endowments from nature' and his lack of practice in civil government."[93] Luckily, President Washington accepted the challenge and successfully led the country in its infantile stages.

According to a study by the *International Journal of Behavioral Science*, the incident rate of impostor syndrome is measured at 70 percent among millennials. CEOs as well as entrepreneurs are also at a

---

[92] Ibid.
[93] Ibid.

higher risk of experiencing impostor syndrome.[94] Chances are, you have

suffered from impostor syndrome at some point in your life, but luckily,

there are ways to overcome the disconcerting feelings that accompany

the affliction. Just as impostor syndrome can lead to natural feelings of

self-doubt, looking at your achievements and failures from different

perspectives can also negate its effects. Instead of automatically giving

the credit for success to others and accepting the blame for failure, look

at the things you did, even if they were small pieces, as part of the

success and perceive failures as a chance to learn.[95] You, and every

other person in life, have experienced failure at one point or another.

Lastly, don't compare your accomplishments or failures against

people within your social network.[96] There will always be someone who

will achieve more than you. Continually focusing on the "what if "can

drive leaders into analysis paralysis where no decision is made, and

sometimes a leader who fails to make a decision fairs far worse than if a

decision had been made.

The impostor syndrome does seem to carry a tangible benefit

---

[94] Kerr, "Why 70% of Millennials Have Impostor Syndrome."
[95] Carter, "Why So Many Millennials Experience Impostor Syndrome."
[96] Ibid.

for leaders, however. "Ironically, people who feel this way are almost always able to meet the requirements of their job, so their fears of inadequacy are just that—fears."[97] George Washington is perceived to be one of the America's greatest presidents, but he always doubted his ability to lead. The impostor syndrome spurred President Washington's determination, and despite the reservations about his ability to lead as president, he turned out to be one of the best leaders the United States has ever had. It is perfectly fine to doubt yourself as a leader just as it is acceptable for you to believe that luck had or will play a part in your success. If you suffer from impostor syndrome, the feelings of inadequacy may never completely disappear, but isn't there a possibility that you might be the leader who your followers perceive you to be? Even if you question your capabilities, there are people who are or who will be counting on you to lead? When that time comes, will impostor syndrome paralyze you or will you be like President Washington and become the leader your followers suspected you to be?

---

[97] Kerr, "Why 70% of Millennials Have Impostor Syndrome."

17. Short Term versus Long Term: How President Ford Came to an Unpopular Decision

Have you ever been in a position where you know that waiting on something will lead to a better result, but instead of waiting, you take the existing result? How quickly do you rationalize your decision? If you self-assessed, would you find that emotion such as desire played a role in seeking immediate gratification?

As a human being, you are not very good at forecasting the future. You frequently discount long-term effects and place more emphasis on the short-term benefits of actions. This is evidenced by a recent survey of chief financial officers at major corporations, when 78 percent of respondents said they were willing to give up "economic value" in order to meet Wall Street's earnings targets. Many of these same CFOs acknowledge the irrationality of such contradictions but, despite recognizing it, would still pursue the short-term gain.[98]

Researchers have found that two distinct areas of the brain compete for control when you try to balance short-term rewards with

---

[98] K. Eisold, "The Power of Short-Term Thinking," *Psychology Today*, May 22, 2014, accessed March 5, 2017, https://www.psychologytoday.com/blog/hidden-motives/201405/the-power-short-term-thinking.

long-term goals. "The study showed that decisions involving the

possibility of immediate reward activated parts of the brain influenced

heavily by neural systems associated with emotion."[99] When reward in

the short term is favorable, your brain seeks to repeat the action or find

some stimulus that can recreate the release of dopamine, a feel-good

chemical in the brain. "The more we enjoy a painless, immediate

reward, the more we want to repeat it."[100] This instant gratification has

an impact on your long-term thinking. "Our emotional brain has a hard

time imagining the future even though our logical brain clearly sees the

future consequences of our current actions."[101]

President Gerald Ford did not expect to become president of

the United States. When Vice-President Spiro Agnew resigned,

President Nixon was told by leading congressional Democrats that

Gerald Ford would be approved by Congress for the position. Ford was

chosen because everyone perceived Ford to be a man of honesty and

[99] S. Schultz, "Study: Brain Battles Itself Over Short-Term Rewards, Long-Term Goals," Office of Communications, Princeton University, October 14, 2004, accessed March 5, 2017, https://www.princeton.edu/pr/news/04/q4/1014-brain.htm.
[100] P. Whybrow, Short-Term Profits Are Bad for Your Brain," *Time*, September 21, 2015, accessed March 5, 2017, http://time.com/4040720/brain-interest-rate/.
[101] Schultz, "Study: Brain Battles Itself Over Short-Term Rewards, Long-Term Goals."

integrity.[102]

On July 24, 1974, the United States Supreme Court ruled in an

8–0 decision that President Nixon had to turn over recordings that

would implicate him in the Watergate scandal. Shortly after this

decision, President Nixon resigned. Prior to doing so, however,

President Nixon sent Alexander Haig, his advisor, to determine if Vice

President Ford would be willing to grant a full pardon to President Nixon

if Nixon were to resign his position. After speaking with his own advisors

and contemplating the decision, Ford re-contacted Haig and indicated

that he would not be willing to pardon President Nixon. Ford came to

the conclusion that such a deal would be tainted and the national

interest would not be served. Despite this belief, President Ford

changed his mind and granted former President Nixon a full pardon on

September 8, 1974. The public outrage was immediate and

vociferous.[103]

Bob Woodward, an investigative reporter who helped break the

Watergate scandal story, pressed President Ford on this decision for

---

[102] J. Cannon, "Gerald R. Ford," PBS, accessed March 3, 2017,
http://www.pbs.org/newshour/spc/character/essays/ford.html.
[103] Ibid.

years trying to figure out what President Ford was thinking when he

ultimately granted former President Nixon the pardon. After many years

of badgering, President Ford explained that a public trial of Nixon would

have prolonged the negativity of the scandal damaging the country even

further. Ultimately, President Ford came to the conclusion that a

presidential pardon was necessary for the country to move forward.

Closure, President Ford believed, was not only what was best for

America but it was also something he needed in order to establish his

own presidency.[104] As could have been expected, many Americans were

outraged by the pardon and this surprised President Ford.

President Ford's decision interestingly reflects both sides of the

short-term versus long-term dilemma. President Ford addressed his

short-term interests in that he was able to establish his own presidency.

What President Ford failed to consider was that citizens would have

trouble focusing on the long-term goal because of the emotional

response that President Nixon's behavior elicited. In order to defeat

your and your followers' natural wiring for short-term satisfaction, you

---

[104] "The Moral Leadership of American Presidents," *Westmont Magazine*, Westmont, College, Summer 2015, accessed March 3, 2017, http://blogs.westmont.edu/magazine/2015/11/30/the-moral-leadership-of-american-presidents/.

need to find some trigger to remind yourself that even favorable decisions have long-term consequences. If you don't, what you see today as the future will quickly become the present, and if you haven't planned properly, there will be consequences for which you, as the leader, will have to take ownership.

18. President Nixon's Risk Appetite

How much risk are you willing to take in your leadership? Would you accept a risky proposition if it meant a huge promotion? What if the risk represented a promotion for one of your followers? Would your risk appetite change? Would you take a significant risk if it meant you could potentially lose your job?

As you get promoted in your organization, you will probably be asked to make decisions that involve not only more risk but also more importance. The heightened levels of risk cause your brain to undergo changes. "Holding power changes brains by boosting testosterone, which in turn increases the chemical messenger dopamine in the brain's rewards systems. Extraordinary power causes extraordinary brain changes, which in their extreme form manifest themselves in personality distortions, such as those seen in dictators like Muammar Gadaffi."[105] The added doses of testosterone and dopamine unconsciously increase your willingness to accept higher levels of risk while also causing you to assess the likelihood of potential positive

---

[105] I. Roberts, "Bankers and the Neuroscience of Greed," *The Guardian*, July 2, 2012, accessed September 1, 2016, https://www.theguardian.com/commentisfree/2012/jul/02/bankers-greed-brain-changes.

outcomes much more favorably.

Research has directly connected power to increased risk-taking by leaders. "Across five studies, we have found converging evidence that a heightened sense of power increases individuals' optimism in viewing risks and their propensity to engage in risky behavior."[106] A leader who has not instituted checks and balances to mitigate the effects of power runs the chance that power and the subsequent increased risk-taking can lead to their demise.

Richard Nixon became president of the United States on January 20, 1969. When the Pentagon Papers, a set of classified documents detailing conduct during the Vietnam War, were leaked to the press, Nixon became irate. Shortly thereafter, President Nixon became consumed by his anger believing that the Democratic Party and the press were conspiring to damage his presidential legacy. President Nixon subsequently sought revenge and was more than eager to use the power of his position to extract what he needed despite the substantial

---

[106] C. Anderson and A. Galinsky, "Power, Optimism, & Risk-Taking," *European Journal of Social Psychology* 36 (2006): 511–36, accessed February 28, 2017, http://citeseerx.ist.psu.edu/viewdoc/download?doi=10.1.1.378.8398&rep=rep1&type=pdf.

risk. Officials in President Nixon's cabinet initiated illegal wiretaps

against American citizens whom they believed to be looking to damage

Nixon's presidency. A group called the "plumbers" orchestrated

burglaries and break-ins trying to find incriminating information against

President Nixon's perceived enemies, which could later be leaked to the

press in order to damage their credibility. Despite his denials, it was

eventually proved that President Nixon knew and approved the illegal

wiretaps, burglaries, and break-ins. Richard Nixon announced he would

resign as president on August 8, 1974.[107]

President Nixon held one of the most powerful positions in the

world, and the psychological changes to his brain caused him to take

unacceptable risks, which led to his downfall. When you make it to the

top of your organization, what will you do to ensure that power doesn't

go to your head?

---

[107] J. Finder, "Call the Plumbers," *New York Times*, November 16, 1997, accessed September 3, 2016, https://www.nytimes.com/books/97/11/16/reviews/971116.16findert. html.

19. How President Eisenhower Circumvented Toxic Personalities

Have you ever been in an organization that possessed a toxic leader at some level of management? How did the toxic leader affect the organizational culture? Did this leader set the wrong tone for the organization? If you're in an organization with a toxic leader, is there anything you can do to improve the culture?

Toxic employees can be harmful to any organization, but they are especially damaging if they hold positional power. If their influence is allowed to grow unchecked, it can poison an entire organization. Unfortunately, the number of toxic leaders in organizations appears to be in a growth stage. Theo Veldsman of the University of Johannesburg has studied toxic leaders and found that about three in every ten leaders in today's organizations are toxic. These individuals take deliberate action to ridicule, undermine, and destroy the self-esteem of others in their organizations.[108]

If not reigned in, toxic leaders can have a lasting effect on

---

[108] R. Williams, "The Rise of Toxic Leadership and Toxic Workplaces," *Psychology Today*, January 27, 2016, accessed August 20, 2016, https://www.psychologytoday.com/blog/wired-success/201601/the-rise-toxic-leadership-and-toxic-workplaces.

organizational culture. "As toxic leaders advance and are rewarded for

their achievements, subordinate leaders are incentivized to adopt their

toxic values as a means of attaining power and promotion."[109] In these

situations, an existing leader or an emerging leader who both have the

best interests of their followers at heart must take control to stop the

downward spiral.

President Eisenhower faced a crisis in September 1957 when

nine African American children attempted to integrate Little Rock

Central High School pursuant to the United States Supreme Court

decision in *Brown v. Board of Education*. On September 2, 1957,

Arkansas governor, Orval Faubus, publicly ordered the Arkansas

National Guard to prevent the nine African American students from

entering the school in direct defiance of the Supreme Court order.

On September 14, 1957, Faubus met with President Eisenhower

where they held discussions about Faubus's actions. President

Eisenhower outlined the Supremacy clause, whereby federal law trumps

state law, and outlined how Faubus could go back to Arkansas and

---

[109] Lt. Col. D. Aubrey, "The Effect of Toxic Leadership," U.S. Army War College, 2012, accessed August 20, 2016, http://www.au.af.mil/au/awc/awcgate/army-usawc/aubrey_toxic_leadership.pdf.

redirect the National Guard to allow the African American children to

attend the school. When Governor Faubus left the meeting with

President Eisenhower, it was Eisenhower's belief that Faubus would

follow through on the president's wishes and the crisis would be over.[110]

    On September 23, 1957, a group of approximately one

thousand angry mobsters entered the Central High School, and Little

Rock Police were forced to escort the nine students out of the building

for their own safety. President Eisenhower struggled with his decision

after Governor Faubus failed to prevent civil unrest. President

Eisenhower expressed great reservation in using military personnel to

restore order, but ultimately, he believed the rule of law to be supreme.

Eisenhower issued a direct order that placed the Arkansas National

Guardsmen under federal control while also sending troops from the

101st Airborne to Little Rock. Central High School was eventually

integrated, peace was restored, and the parents of the nine children

---

[110] D. Eisenhower, "President Eisenhower's Diary," Eisenhower Library,
October 8, 1957, accessed August 20, 2016,
https://www.eisenhower.archives.gov/research/online_documents/civil
_rights_little_rock/1957_10_08_Diary_Notes_Faubus_Meeting.pdf.

sent a telegram thanking President Eisenhower for his actions.[111]

Governor Faubus was a toxic leader who emboldened his followers to openly revoke a United States Supreme Court decision. He also used his powers as governor to create dissonance within the minds of the National Guardsmen who were conflicted by doing what was right and obeying a direct order from their leader. "Research suggests that the behavior of toxic leaders may serve to rationalize or excuse negative behavior in the group and establish a new 'toxic' set of norms."[112] President Eisenhower refused to allow the new norms to be accepted when he issued his order placing the National Guardsmen under control of the US government. If you serve a toxic leader or you allow toxic leaders to rule in your organization, what steps are you taking to ensure that your followers don't have to suffer while working for a toxic leader?

---

[111] D. Eisenhower, "Civil Rights: The Little Rock School integration Crisis," Eisenhower Library, 1957, accessed August 20, 2016, https://www.eisenhower.archives.gov/research/online_documents/civil _rights_little_rock.html.
[112] Aubrey, "The Effect of Toxic Leadership."

20. President Kennedy's Fork in the Road: Leadership and Accountability

Can you recall a pivotal moment in your life where you were faced with a decision that could potentially dictate how your career or even your life progressed? When faced with this decision, did you consider all factors such as career, family, and health? Once you made the decision, would you be willing to accept the ramifications if things went wrong?

You probably believe that when making a decision, you follow the rational choice theory in which you objectively weigh the costs and benefits associated with either outcome. Normally you would choose the option that maximizes what you desire. However, there are a number of things that affect your decision-making ability in ways that you do not consciously recognize. For example, studies have shown how your mood affects your decision-making ability. "When you're in a negative mood, you tend to expect more negative outcomes and see yourself and others more negatively."[113] Even though you believe you have made a completely rational decision,

---

[113] K. Hall, "A Few of the Many Ways We Distort Reality," *Psychology Today*, August 30, 2012, accessed January 14, 2017, https://www.psychologytoday.com/blog/pieces-mind/201208/few-the-many-ways-we-distort-reality.

your brain has processed the information in such a way that your

biases go unnoticed.

Luckily, the ramifications from your bad or incorrect decisions

can be minimal or nonexistent. Sometimes, however, your failures

are very public. When this occurs, you will have to try to go against

your brain's natural desire to look favorably upon your actions. A

bad outcome causes cognitive dissonance as well as stress in your

body because your actions (believing that you made a good decision)

do not reconcile with the results.[114] This dissonance leads to you

being reluctant to admit failure.

In 1959, Fidel Castro became the leader of the Cuban

government and a threat to the United States when Castro

immediately leveraged his new position to establish relations with

the Soviet Union. With the Soviet Union having influence in a country

perilously close to the United States, President Kennedy approved a

plan to train approximately fourteen hundred Cuban dissidents to

invade Cuba and overthrow Castro's government. Shortly before

midnight on April 16, 1961, the raid began in the Bay of Pigs, but

[114] L. Holmes, "Why It's So Hard To Admit When You're Wrong," *Huffington Post*, October 2, 2015, accessed January 14, 2017, http://www.huffingtonpost.com/entry/just-say-sorry-matt_us_560c29d1e4b0af3706df0ee8.

Cuban soldiers immediately routed the trained dissidents.[115] It was a

tremendous failure for President Kennedy and represented a fork in

the road on his leadership journey. President Kennedy could have

easily spun the facts of what happened into something less

embarrassing to mute his cognitive dissonance and balance his

innate need to see himself as a good person, or he could be confident

enough to admit his errors knowing that one bad decision does not

necessarily make him a bad person. In his speech to the nation,

President Kennedy said the following, "Ladies and gentlemen.

Success has a thousand followers and failure is an orphan. I failed.

Blame me."[116]

How you handle your failures and your mistakes are important

to followers. Leaders who are willing to admit to shortcomings earn

respect and trust while also setting the organizational culture.

"When leaders admit to mistakes, it brings clarity to opportunity

gaps and elevates a deeper sense of accountability that can be shared

---

[115] M. Voss, "Bay of Pigs: The 'Perfect Failure' of Cuba Invasion," BBC, April 14, 2011, accessed January 14, 2017, http://www.bbc.com/news/world-latin-america-13066561.
[116] T. Fox, "What Makes a President a Great Leader," *Washington Post*, November 6, 2012, accessed January 14, 2017, https://www.washingtonpost.com/national/on-leadership/what-makes-a-president-a-great-leader/2012/11/06/2f0ef12c-2825-11e2-96b6-8e6a7524553f_story.html?utm_term=.922d662c81dd.

amongst the team."[117] In addition, failures and mistakes are an

important part of any leadership journey. Sometimes, as President

Kennedy did, you learn better lessons from failing than from

succeeding. "Kennedy stood up to it, took the blame for the Bay of

Pigs, rearranged his staff and a year later when confronted by the

Cuban Missile Crisis steered a steady and successful course through

that nuclear peril."[118]

Followers appreciated President Kennedy's willingness to

accept responsibility as a leader and his approval ratings soared

post-incident.[119] The next time you reach a fork in the road on your

leadership journey, are you going to bend to those deep-seated

psychological desires to maintain your favorable self-perception or

are you going to hold yourself accountable...just like you would any

of your followers?

---

[117] S. Llopis, "4 Reasons Great Leaders Admit Their Mistakes," *Forbes*, July 23, 2015, accessed January 14, 2017, http://www.forbes.com/sites/glennllopis/2015/07/23/4-reasons-great-leaders-admit-their-mistakes/2/#667e59367295.

[118] H. Sidey, The Lesson John Kennedy Learned from the Bay of Pigs," *Time*, April 16, 2001, accessed January 14, 2017, http://content.time.com/time/nation/article/0,8599,106537,00.html.

[119] T. Fox, "What Makes a President a Great Leader,"

21. President Truman's Unpopular Decision

How many leaders have you had in your career who knew what the right decision was but failed to follow through because they knew the decision wouldn't be popular? Did that decision ever come back to haunt the leader? How have you fared as a leader when a difficult decision arose? Were you brave enough to make the correct decision despite popular opinion?

Throughout history, we have valued the leaders who put forth courageous efforts as well as those who fought through adversity. In these instances, the leaders usually went against the grain and did things other people were unable or unwilling to do. Taking action in these moments required a willingness to take great risk as, most of the time, the leader would choose a path that the majority had forsaken. Jack Zenger studied bold leadership and found that leaders who possessed good judgment but were not bold had a 1 percent chance of becoming an extraordinary leader. Leaders who were bold but possessed bad judgment had a 4 percent chance of being an extraordinary leader. Leaders who possessed good judgment and were also perceived as bold had a 95 percent chance of becoming an extraordinary leader.[120]

Group behavior can be very powerful, and a leader who is willing to go against collective opinions and behaviors can experience unease. If you recognize the need to do what others won't, you are likely to face immediate criticism and ridicule from other group members or peers who would prefer the status quo. The derision expressed by others can originate deep in the human psyche. "Though some people thrive on a new set of challenges, others wince and feel vulnerable. Change, for them, means learning new skills and giving up stuff they are great at. Change may challenge their competency."[121] Moving from a position of competence to one of inexperience can be damaging to self-confidence and lead to the familiar plea, "But is this the way we've always done it?"

If you, as the leader, were to continually accept the status quo, you would be stifling innovation in your organization. Change causes stress

---

[120] J. Folkman, "Bold Leadership: The Four Steps That Take Leaders to Another Level," *Fortune*, June 18, 2015, accessed April 15, 2017, https://www.forbes.com/sites/joefolkman/2015/06/18/bold-leadership-the-4-steps-that-take-leaders-to-another-level/#21de14085cfa.

[121] S. Bacharach, "4 Reasons Your Employees Resist Change—And How to Overcome Them," Inc., April 17, 2013, accessed April 14, 2017, https://www.inc.com/samuel-bacharach/four-reasons-your-employees-resist-change-and-how-to-overcome-them.html.

and anxiety, however, and that affects how you perceive things. "Stress makes us prone to tunnel vision, less likely to take in the information we need. Anxiety makes us more risk-averse than we would be regularly and more deferential."[122]

Leading change by making difficult, unpopular decisions may cause stress in your followers, but if you can maintain your vision, the future could be brighter for all. "Standing behind decisions everyone supports doesn't particularly require a lot of chutzpa. On the other hand, standing behind what one believes is the right decision in the face of tremendous controversy is the stuff great leaders are made of."[123]

General Douglas MacArthur was a celebrated war veteran and a well-known war hero when North Korea invaded South Korea in the 1950s. President Truman placed MacArthur in command and MacArthur proceeded to drive the North Koreans back to the borders of China. With such exploits, MacArthur's heroic image grew even brighter.

---

[122] N. Hertz, "Why We Make Bad Decisions," *New York Times*, October 19, 2013, accessed October 27, 2017, http://www.nytimes.com/2013/10/20/opinion/sunday/why-we-make-bad-decisions.html.
[123] M. Myatt, "Every Great Leader Has This Quality—Do You?," *Forbes*, September 19, 2012, accessed October 27, 2016, http://www.forbes.com/sites/mikemyatt/2012/09/19/every-great-leader-has-this-quality-do-you/#2d9124f123b7.

As MacArthur pushed the North Koreans back, it drew China into the war. President Truman became concerned about the escalating conflict and desired to keep it from spiraling out of control. General MacArthur, on the other hand, had a different perspective and requested permission from President Truman to expand the war campaign toward China. President Truman abruptly refused. MacArthur responded to President Truman's decision by going directly to the United States Congress as well as the media to state his case for advancement into China.

Despite MacArthur's extreme popularity, President Truman not only continued to deny MacArthur's request but also eventually removed MacArthur from his command at the height of his popularity. Truman sent a message to all of his followers that he was the one in charge.[124] If followers were willing to try and go around him, there would be consequences. President Truman was willing to make an unpopular stand because he believed that any escalation of the war would bring more casualties as well as bring a greater threat to

---

[124] J. Venable, "4 Examples of Extraordinary Presidential Leadership," The Daily Signal, February 15, 2016, accessed October 9, 2016, http://dailysignal.com/2016/02/15/4-examples-of-extraordinary-presidential-leadership/.

worldwide peace. By making this difficult decision, President Truman reaffirmed his position as commander in chief and reinforced the strength of the presidency.

Making difficult decisions that cause change in organizations is something you will inevitably have to face. While it would be easier for you to reaffirm the status quo, you must fight against the group and social pressures to forego change at the expense of improving the organization. "It takes courage to break from the norm, to work in collaboration, not isolation, challenge the status quo, seek new opportunities, cut your losses, make the tough decision, listen rather than speak, admit your faults, forgive the faults of others, not allow failure to dampen your spirit, stand for those not capable of standing for themselves and to remain true to your core values."[125] In order for a transformation to take place, you must stay true to your convictions when the cascades of criticism fall from those who simply want to avoid the stress that comes with change. Many people who mask themselves as leaders will succumb to group opinion, but the great leaders find ways to share their vision and lead through the natural discomfort of

---

[125] Myatt, "Every Great Leader Has This Quality."

change. As you look at yourself today, are you bold enough to make the

decisions required of an extraordinary leader?

22. President Teddy Roosevelt Takes an Ethical Stand

When it comes time to make an ethical decision, where do you look for guidance? Do you recall all the lessons you have learned through life, believing that the guidance you seek lies in a past event? Do you look to religion for an answer? Would you take into account the things your friends or peers have done in similar situations? Would you seek the greater good for the greatest number of people?

Ethics can be derived from many places, including how you were raised, religion, past experiences, laws, and environment. Societal standards and even wealth (or the lack of it) can make a difference in your ethical decision-making processes. These perspectives help a leader to choose what is wrong and what is right. All leaders, however, won't make the same choices given similar circumstances.

Recently, researchers from the University of California, Berkeley and the University of Toronto studied the ethical tendencies of people from a variety of socioeconomic backgrounds. Their findings were somewhat surprising. "Those with an upper-class background were more likely to break the rules and the law."[126] Perspectives derived from

life experiences can have an impact on our view of the world. Leaders

are no different. If leaders perceive themselves to have earned certain

status or privileges, their ethical decision making is impacted as

evidenced by a test involving wealthy motorists and pedestrians.

"Upper-class motorists were three times more willing to cut pedestrians

off at an intersection and four times more likely to cut off other vehicles

at a busy four-way intersection."[127] Their behavior didn't stop with

motorists, however. "The fourth experiment involved assigning the

volunteers a task in the library where there was a jar of candy reserved

for visiting children. Invited to take a candy or two for themselves,

upper-class volunteers helped themselves to twice as much candy as

the other volunteers did."[128] If asked, it is doubtful that any of these

leaders would openly state they would steal from children, but

sometimes leaders become accustomed to getting what they want and

act accordingly.

---

[126] N. Wagner, "Are Rich People More Ethical?," *The Atlantic*, March 24, 2012, accessed October 24, 2016, http://www.theatlantic.com/health/archive/2012/03/are-rich-people-more-ethical/254689/.
[127] Ibid.
[128] Ibid.

When John Stumpf and others at Wells Fargo created the sales

incentive program "Eight is Great," they probably didn't consider the

idea that employees who were pressured to meet sales goals would

misuse their customers' information. Their perspective and experiences

allowed them to believe that the bank was generating the revenue from

legitimate sources when, in fact, immigrants who spoke little English,

older and younger customers, as well as small business owners were

paying fees for products they didn't need.[129]

If a leader can keep him- or herself grounded and maintain the

perspective of those outside their normal social circles, there is the

chance that a better ethical decision can be made. Theodore Roosevelt

became president of the United States just as the economy moved from

an agrarian basis to an industrial basis. As such, there were entities

ready to take advantage of the change. With no precedence or laws in

place to protect them, industry was like the Wild West taking shortcuts

in regards to worker safety as well as product safety and employing

monopolistic practices to artificially inflate market prices. President

---

[129] S. Cowley, "'Lions Hunting Zebras': Ex-Wells Fargo Bankers Describe Abuses," CNBC, October 21, 2016, accessed October 24, 2016, http://www.cnbc.com/2016/10/21/new-york-times-lions-hunting-zebras-ex-wells-fargo-bankers-describe-abuses.html.

Roosevelt promised the electorate a "Square Deal" in that he believed

everyone, not just those with wealth, should get a fair chance at

opportunity.[130]

Roosevelt backed up his promise by getting Congress to pass

the Elkins Act and Hepburn Act, which regulated shipping costs so that

favored parties would not get preferred deals that an ordinary citizen

could not get. In addition, President Roosevelt fervently pursued

violations of the Sherman Antitrust Act, and after publication of *The*

Jungle by Upton Sinclair, Roosevelt was instrumental in leading the

charge to pass the Meat Inspection Act and the Food and Drug Act,

which placed controls and required inspections of meat-packing plants

as well as other foods and medicines.[131] By pursuing the "Square Deal,"

President Roosevelt ensured that the ordinary American citizen was just

as important as the wealthy American businessman.

At the time that President Roosevelt was making these

decisions, the American economy was growing. It would have been easy

---

[130] Source: Boundless. "The Square Deal," *Boundless U.S. History*, Boundless, June 28, 2016, accessed September 17, 2016, https//www.boundless.com/u-s-history/textbooks/boundless-u-s-history-textbook/the-progressive-era-1890-1917-22/Roosevelt-s-progressivism-1434/the-square-deal-1437-1243/
[131] Ibid.

for President Roosevelt to ignore the pleas of the workingman in the

name of progress, but he chose to act. President Roosevelt understood

the relation of ethics to perspective and made sure that he remained

grounded even as he ascended to one of the most powerful positions in

the world. As President Roosevelt's actions showed, people who serve

their leader are entitled to service by their leader.

23. President Carter at Camp David

Have you ever attempted to resolve a conflict between two

parties? How was your experience? Did you find the process frustrating

or did you enjoy trying to bridge the gap between the parties? What

would happen if something very important to your organization hinged

upon you helping two parties reach an agreement?

Conflict arises when two people or parties see the same

circumstances but believe in different solutions. Ideally, these

differences would be solved through collaboration, but sometimes

perceptions and emotions prevent any meaningful collaboration. In the

workplace, you, as the leader, are often expected to step in and help

resolve the conflict.

It is important for you to remember that conflict resolution is a

process. Many parties involved in a conflict have established social

identities, which are exclusive of each other allowing one party to

determine themselves as the "us," while categorizing the other party as

the "them." "Examination of the way in which group attitudes and

perspectives feed, escalate, and perpetuate intergroup conflict can

provide conceptual tools to overcome the subjective factors such as psychological barriers that set constraint on rationality in resolving

conflicts."[132]

A characteristic of conflict resolution is a party's resistance to

change even in the face of contradictory information. Confirmation bias

leads the parties to see only the items that support their original

position and to ignore data that threatens their position. This is a

natural reaction to cognitive dissonance, but because of this, you must

develop means to help yourself and others to overcome these social

psychological behaviors in order to reach consensus.

Conflicts between parties are not always based on rational

thought. Emotions can lead us to provoke behaviors in our counterparts

that fulfill preconceived notions. "Self-fulfilling prophecies arise when a

party's expectations about their adversary cause them to act in ways

that actually provoke the adversary's 'expected' response."[133] If you are

attempting to resolve conflict, you have to get the parties to understand

---

[132] H. Kelman, "Conflict Resolution & Reconciliation: A Social-Psychological Perspective on Ending Violent Conflict Between Identity Groups," *Landscapes of Violence, An Interdisciplinary Journal Devoted to the Study of Violence, Conflict and Trauma* 1, no. 1 (2010): Article 5, October 1, 2010, accessed September 3, 2016, http://www.socialinquiry.org/articles/IJSI-V4N12011%20-%20010.pdf.
[133] Ibid.

the issue from each other's perspective, all the while trying to keep the emotion out of the issue.

One way for you to start building a collective social identity is to stress the positive versus the negative. In almost every negotiation, there are certain items that both parties agree upon. "Prior to negotiations, the mediator should prepare a document stating all the points on which the parties agree."[134] By highlighting these items and showing the commonalities, you can start to bridge the chasm between the two parties and in some cases show that there are more things the parties agree with than they oppose.

Because it is easier to continue with the status quo, there will be times when a party will want to abandon any attempt at resolution. If that were to occur, you might benefit from explaining what would or could happen if the party left the negotiation. If you can convince the party that the alternative solution would be worse if they left than if they stayed, it might be enough to keep them in the resolution process. "In business negotiations, pressuring someone to stay at the table can

---

[134] T. Glaser, *A Conversation on Peacemaking with Jimmy Carter* (Washington, DC: National Institute for Dispute Resolution, 1992), accessed September 3, 2016, http://www.colorado.edu/conflict/peace/example/acon7268.htm.

be unwise and unprofessional. But by reminding an obstinate party of the potential of negative consequences of their departure, you may be able to persuade them to try a bit harder."[135]

In 1978, Israeli prime minister Menachem Begin and Egyptian president Anwar Sadat arrived at Camp David, Maryland, at the invitation of US president Jimmy Carter. Carter hoped to facilitate a peace treaty between Israel and Egypt but quickly found that he would have to play a more active role when it became apparent that Sadat and Begin weren't ready to negotiate directly. President Carter quickly took on the new role and bounced back and forth between the parties helping them to understand each other's perspectives while also highlighting the collective interests of both parties. President Carter provided almost daily updates on polling data in the respective nations, showing the people's will for an agreement to be made. He reminded Sadat of their friendship and personally addressed pictures to eight of Begin's grandchildren after receiving a direct request from Begin.[136]

---

[135] K. Shonk, "In Conflict Resolution, President Carter Turned Flaws Into Virtues," Harvard Program on Negotiation Daily Blog, Harvard Law School, 2008, accessed September 3, 2016, http://www.pon.harvard.edu/daily/conflict-resolution/in-conflict-resolution-president-carter-turned-flaws-into-virtues/.
[136] Glaser, *A Conversation On Peacemaking With Jimmy Carter.*

When Begin threatened to leave Camp David without an agreement in

place, Carter told Begin he would instruct his aides to draft a speech

asking Israelis to vote down their government if Begin followed through

on his threat to leave. President Carter physically blocked the door

when President Sadat threatened to return to Egypt and promised to

isolate Egypt from the rest of the world if Sadat did, in fact, leave Camp

David.[137] Finally on September 18, 1978, a peace agreement between

Israeli Prime Minister Begin and Egyptian President Sadat was

announced publicly.[138]

President Carter walked the fine line of conflict resolution by

ensuring that each party saw the other party's perspective without

falling into certain biases and emotions, which could have damaged the

resolution process at any point in time. As you seek resolution in conflict

management, you must fight through the resistance to change and try

to create a social identity that encompasses each party's interests. The

next time you try to resolve a conflict, will you be able to adapt to the

---

[137] "How Can You Resolve a Heated Conflict in Your Workplace," Harvard Program on Negotiation Daily Blog, Harvard Law School, 2008, accessed September 3, 2016, http://www.pon.harvard.edu/daily/conflict-resolution/in-conflict-resolution-president-carter-turned-flaws-into-virtues/.
[138] Shonk, "In Conflict Resolution, President Carter Turned Flaws Into Virtues."

needs of the negotiating party as President Carter did?

24. The Value of an Honest Leader

Do you consider yourself to be an honest leader? Are you ready

and willing to state the uncomfortable truth to a follower, albeit in a

tactful way? Do you dread these types of conversations? If you were to

turn the equation around, how did you feel when your leader gave you

an honest assessment of where you stood in your organization? Was it

difficult to accept? In the long run, did the unfiltered, honest message

help or hurt your growth?

Whether you know it or not, followers crave honesty, even the kind

that makes them uncomfortable. "Honesty is a leader's most valued and

valuable leadership quality because it is the gateway for trust and

inspiration."[139] Without trust, there is no true leader-follower

relationship. In fact, trust is the most valued quality in leaders (89

percent) per a survey of over one hundred thousand people as

conducted by Jim Kouzes and Barry Posner.[140]

If honesty is so important to leadership, why is it that so many

---

[139] M. Bunting, "Honesty: The Single Most Important Leadership Value," *CEO Magazine*, March 4, 2016, accessed February 28, 2017, http://www.theceomagazine.com/business/honesty-the-single-most-important-leadership-value/.
[140] J. M. Kouzes and B. Z. Posner, *The Leadership Challenge* (San Francisco: Jossey-Bass, 2003).

employees feel like their positional leaders are being dishonest with

them? Edelman, a public-relations firm, conducts a trust barometer

survey every year. In 2014, they found that only 20 percent of people

trust business leaders and only 13 percent of people trust government

leaders.[141] The 2017 Edelman Trust Barometer survey rated CEO

credibility at their lowest levels ever.[142]

Honesty by leaders, or lack thereof, can be the root problem of any

number of organizational issues. "Managers sometimes believe that

access to information is a perquisite of power, a benefit that separates

their privileged caste from the unwashed hoi polloi."[143] By withholding

information unnecessarily, you can place your leadership in jeopardy if

your followers perceive that you are not being forthright because of

ulterior motives or because you see information as a tool to exploit

while retaining positional superiority.

In the late 1880s, Grover Cleveland was elected mayor of Buffalo

---

[141] Bunting, "Honesty: The Single Most Important Leadership Value."
[142] "2017 Trust Barometer Reveals Global Implosion of Trust," Edelman, January 15, 2017, accessed February 28, 2017, http://www.edelman.com/news/2017-edelman-trust-barometer-reveals-global-implosion/.
[143] J. O'Toole and W. Bennis, "A Culture of Candor," *Harvard Business Review*, June 2009, accessed February 28, 2017, https://hbr.org/2009/06/a-culture-of-candor.

and immediately took city aldermen to task for accepting kickbacks on

public contracts. Shortly thereafter, Cleveland was recruited to run for

governor of New York, where he fired government employees on the

take and launched public investigations into graft and corruption.

Ordinary American citizens who were tired of government officials using

their positions to enrich themselves were happy when the Democratic

Party made Cleveland their presidential nominee in 1884.[144]

As the election neared, a bit of dirty laundry was discovered about

Grover Cleveland; he had apparently fathered a child out of wedlock. As

the story gained traction in newspapers, political strategists discussed

the best way to manage the incriminating information. Cleveland's

response was simple and in the form of a telegram to his campaign

officials, "Whatever you do, tell the truth."[145] Cleveland was also given

derogatory material about his presidential competitor. After receiving

an envelope containing the incriminating information, Cleveland,

without looking inside, tore the envelope to bits and burned it in the

---

[144] J. Jacoby, "'Grover The Good'—The Most Honest President of All," Boston Globe, February 15, 2015, accessed February 28, 2017, https://www.bostonglobe.com/opinion/2015/02/15/presidents-day-grover-cleveland-most-honest-president-them-all/CmhndHa3aA1t0cvAfjB6LL/story.html.
[145] Ibid.

fireplace.[146]

Grover Cleveland would go on to become US president in 1884 and then again in 1892. President Cleveland would become the master of the veto, sending back congressional bills 414 times in his first term alone. This figure was more than double of all the presidents who had preceded him. President Cleveland would not compromise his position as the steward of taxpayer money and followed through with his convictions concerning political favors. His honesty and openness led to a public trust and admiration that is hard for leaders to attain.[147]

Honesty by leaders has a direct and meaningful impact on your follower's behavior, motivation, and engagement. "Leaders with high perceived behavioral integrity lead teams that are significantly more satisfied in their job, are less likely to be absent, less stressed, and report greater overall health and wellbeing and life satisfaction."[148] Can you follow President Cleveland's example and be honest in difficult

---

[146] D. Lythgoe, "America's Calling Grover Cleveland. We Need an Honest Man in The Oval Office," *Deseret News*, January 22, 1999, accessed February 28, 2017, http://www.deseretnews.com/article/675903/Americas-calling-Grover-Cleveland.html.
[147] Jacoby, "Grover The Good."
[148] Bunting, "Honesty: The Single Most Important Leadership Value."

times? Your leadership credibility may depend upon your ability to do

so.

25. Social Status and the Relation to Leadership

Have you ever had to remind yourself that other people's opinions don't necessarily matter? Yet despite this warning, you probably still fall into an emotional abyss when someone you respected criticized one of your decisions. Why do other people's opinions matter so much? Have you ever let the criticism affect your future decisions? How does this affect you as a leader?

Whether you realize it or not, your social status weighs heavily on your decision-making process. "Nobel Laureate economist, John Haranyi, said that apart from economic payoffs, social status seems to be the most important incentive and motivating source of social behavior."[149] Frequently, your social status is derived from what your perceived peers think about you, and that is why you are continually seeking reaffirmation from those whom you consider to be in your peer group. "We rarely pause to consider what others might think when the context is good because we're assured that our status within the group is unaffected. And negative opinions held by those outside of our social groups may have less weight than others because they are less likely to

---

[149] A. Waytz, "The Psychology of Social Status," *Scientific American*, December 8, 2009, accessed July 7, 2017, https://www.scientificamerican.com/article/the-psychology-of-social/.

have an impact on our future relations. It is only when our social

standing is threatened that we begin to wonder...what are people going

to think?"[150]

President George Washington held future President Thomas

Jefferson in such high esteem that Jefferson was appointed America's

first secretary of state. While the two men worked well together

preindependence, governing the new republic led to philosophical

differences. Washington chose to support Federalists, who advocated a

strong central government focusing on commerce, while Jefferson

preferred the states to have more power and to focus on an agrarian

economy. These disagreements frayed the trust and confidence

between the two men, and Jefferson resigned his position in 1793.

Washington later learned that Jefferson had written a defamatory letter

to a friend in which Jefferson criticized his former colleagues, none of

whom were named. When Washington found out about this letter, he

assumed, rightly or wrongly, Jefferson was speaking directly about him.

Communication ceased between the two leaders at this point. President

---

[150] K. D'Costa, "What Other People Think About Us Matters Here's Why," *Scientific American*, June 4, 2012, accessed July 7, 2017, https://blogs.scientificamerican.com/anthropology-in-practice/what-other-people-think-about-us-mattersheres-why/.

Washington's disdain for Jefferson was clearly evident when Martha Washington referred to President Jefferson's election as, "The greatest misfortune our country has ever experienced."[151]

President Washington, during his terms as president, likely had others questioning his decision making, but what made Jefferson's criticism different was that President Washington considered Jefferson to be of the same social status and in his peer group. If you look back in your life, did criticism sting more if it came from someone who you admired or trusted versus from someone you barely knew?

Oftentimes as a leader, you attribute certain facts and ideas to other people's statements that aren't necessarily based in truth. "Part of the problem is we all tend to believe we see things as they are. That there's sort of a one-to-one relationship between what you're doing and what I'm seeing. The reality is actually there's what you're doing and then there's a whole bunch of other stuff that gets put into the mix in your brain, very much unconsciously, to lend meaning to what you're

---

[151] A. Crawford, "Once Allies, Politics Served to Fracture the Relationships of These Founding Fathers from Virginia," George Washington's Mount Vernon, unknown date, accessed August 1, 2016, http://www.mountvernon.org/george-washington/the-first-president/washington-jefferson-madison/.

doing."[152] President Washington likely judged Jefferson's criticism to be a personal attack because of their previous philosophical disagreements, even though there was no direct reference to President Washington in the letter.

You, like President Washington, make instantaneous, subconscious decisions about people based on your beliefs, your life experiences, and your previous interactions. Frequently, these initial impressions are correct, but what if they aren't? Is it possible that you could mistakenly perceive something one of your peers or followers did or said? The next time you find yourself bothered by something someone said or did, look deep inside to see if you should truly be angered or if you are simply trying to preserve your social standing in your peer group.

---

[152] S. Green, "Understand How People See You," *Harvard Business Review*, April 16, 2015, accessed July 8, 2017, https://hbr.org/ideacast/2015/04/understand-how-people-see-you.html.

Get Off Your Horse! Fifty-two Succinct Leadership Lessons From US Presidents

26. President Johnson and Grandiose Narcissism

Have you ever worked for a positional leader who was completely full of him- or herself? Did they allow anything to get in the way of their ambition? What happened when you offered advice contrary to what this type of leader desired? Would you like working for a leader who was more interested in his or her own advancement even at the expense of his or her followers?

From the beginning of time, leadership has been populated by a fair share of narcissists. Narcissism among US presidents has been steadily on the rise according to W. Keith Campbell. Based on Campbell's study, certain presidents have possessed massive egos. The most narcissistic US presidents, according to Campbell's study, were Lyndon B. Johnson, followed by Teddy Roosevelt, Andrew Jackson, Franklin Roosevelt, John F. Kennedy, and Richard Nixon.[153]

Grandiosity, entitlement, and a lack of empathy are hallmark traits of narcissism. Grandiosity leads you to believe that you are better than everyone else while entitlement prompts you to believe that you are

---

[153] B. Boland, "Narcissism Part of Presidential Job Description, Professor Says," CNS News, January 24, 2014, accessed October 27, 2016, http://www.cnsnews.com/news/article/barbara-boland/narcissism-part-presidential-job-description-professor-says.

more deserving. A lack of empathy leads you to indifference when interacting with your followers.[154] The behaviors exhibited by each person are dependent upon how deeply ingrained the narcissism is into the person's personality.

Increased narcissism among the population is a growing trend for the near future. The incidence of narcissistic personality disorder is nearly three times as high for people in their twenties as to the generation that's now sixty-five or older, according to the National Institutes of Health. In addition, 58 percent more college students scored higher on a narcissism scale in 2009 than in 1982.[155] Even so, there are good sides and bad sides to having narcissists as leaders. Sigmund Freud once wrote this about narcissists, "They are especially suited to act as a support for others, to take on the role of leaders, and to give a fresh stimulus to cultural development or damage the

---

[154] J. Kluger, "Why Narcissists Become President, with Jeffrey Kluger," Big Think, 2015, accessed November 12, 2016, http://bigthink.com/think-tank/why-narcissists-get-elected-president-with-jeffrey-kluger.
[155] Boland, "Narcissism Part of Presidential Job Description, Professor Says."

established state of affairs."[156]

Lyndon B. Johnson became the US president in 1963 after President John F Kennedy was assassinated. Johnson had openly aspired to be the greatest president in history but eventually made a calculated decision to become President Kennedy's vice president when he felt that he would not be able to maintain his measurable power and status as the majority leader of the Senate. Johnson planned on transforming the vice president's job into a much more important position than what his predecessors had done. His attempts to grab power were largely ignored or dismissed by President Kennedy. President Kennedy did desire, however, to keep Johnson happy and busy. As such, Johnson traveled the world as a representative and voice for President Kennedy's worldwide vision.[157]

Johnson's narcissism, although widely known by President Kennedy, was reflected in these trips as well as in other instances.

---

[156] M. Maccoby, "Narcissistic Leaders: The Incredible Pros; The Inevitable Cons," *Harvard Business Review*, January 2004, accessed October 27, 2016, https://hbr.org/2004/01/narcissistic-leaders-the-incredible-pros-the-inevitable-cons.
[157] R. Dallek, "Flawed Giant, Lyndon Johnson and His Times 1961–1973," *The New York Times*, 1998, accessed November 12, 2016, http://www.nytimes.com/books/first/d/dallek-giant.html.

When President Johnson traveled to Senegal in April 1961, he requested

a seven-foot bed, a special shower head that emitted a needle-point

spray, cases of Cutty Sark, and boxes of ballpoint pens and cigarette

lighters with the initials "L. B. J." inscribed on each of them. On the

same worldwide trip, Johnson stopped in Bangkok and held a press

conference in his pajamas to address misinformation printed in a

newspaper.[158] Johnson exhibited other behaviors that were based in his

narcissism. He once urinated on a Secret Service agent who was

shielding Johnson from public view and told the surprised Secret Service

agent that it was his presidential prerogative to do so. President

Johnson ensured that his children and even his dog had the same initials

as him, and he insisted that his initials were embroidered on his bath

towels.[159] Despite these foibles, President Johnson is still ranked as the

twelfth most effective US president in history.[160]

---

[158] Ibid.

[159] J. Drapkin, "LBJ: The President Who Marked His Territory," Mental Floss, April 18, 2008, accessed November 12, 2016, http://mentalfloss.com/article/18463/lbj-president-who-marked-his-territory.

[160] B. Rottinghaus and J. Vaughn, "New Ranking of U.S. Presidents Puts Lincoln At No. 1, Obama At 18; Kennedy Judged Most Overrated," *The Washington Post*, February 16, 2015, accessed November 12, 2016, https://www.washingtonpost.com/news/monkey-

Striving for excellence is by no means a negative trait. How we

choose to reach levels of excellence is where our egos can misdirect us.

Having narcissistic traits can propel leaders to greater heights, but they

are equally as likely to destroy a leader's credibility. "Narcissistic leaders

are less likely to engage in pro-social organizational behavior and more

likely to cheat and violate integrity standards. Narcissistic leaders are

more likely to have unhappy employees and create destructive

workplaces."[161] Even the most narcissistic of leaders must remember

one thing...followers can choose who they want as their leader.

---

cage/wp/2015/02/16/new-ranking-of-u-s-presidents-puts-lincoln-1-obama-18-kennedy-judged-most-over-rated/.
[161] C. O'Reilly, B. Doerr, D. Caldwell, and J. Chatman, "Narcissistic Leaders and Executive Compensation," Leadership Quarterly, 2013, accessed April 15, 2017, http://haas.berkeley.edu/faculty/papers/chatman_narcissism.pdf.

27. Attracting Followers: President Jackson and the 1828 Election

Have you ever seen a person who just naturally draws people to

them? Does it seem that this person becomes the leader without even

trying? Do you ever wonder how they attract followers so easily? Are

there attributes that you can learn from these natural born leaders and

implement them into your leadership style?

There are thousands upon thousands of articles on leadership, but

rarely do these articles address a leader's most critical need...followers.

Without followers, there are no leaders. "What most analyses seem to

ignore, though, is that followers have their own identity."[162] As such,

followers ultimately decide who they want their leader to be. Their

choices normally reflect their own life experiences, values, and culture.

In some instances, followers, whose values align with other people they

consider to be in-group members, may accept the leadership choice

made by their perceived peers. More often than not, however, you

transfer your values onto the leader you choose, which enables your

---

[162] M. Maccoby, "Why People Follow The Leader: The Power of Transference," *Harvard Business Review*, September 2004, accessed October 7, 2016, https://hbr.org/2004/09/why-people-follow-the-leader-the-power-of-transference.

chosen leader to appear to have similar traits as you.

However, science has shown that your implicit biases may limit

the effectiveness of your choices. "A big part of the problem is that we

really don't know how to pick good leaders, due to psychological biases

and trying to serve our own self-interests, rather than the greater

good."[163] Once you have transferred your values onto your leader, you

then look quite differently at that leader. You are more willing to

tolerate immoral and illegal behavior because you now share a social

identity, which you have helped create. Blindly accepting the vision of

the leader because you have identified with him or her can lead to

troubling results.

In the 1940s, Dr. Stanley Milgram did an experiment involving

ordinary people and their willingness to use electric shock as a

punishment for people who could not answer test questions correctly.

Many of the study participants were willing to shock their test subjects

at levels that would have easily killed the other person. While Milgram

believed the willingness to deliver fatal doses of shock was based on an

---

[163] R. Riggio, "5 Reasons We Follow Bad Leaders," *Psychology Today*, July 10, 2016, accessed October 7, 2016, https://www.psychologytoday.com/blog/cutting-edge-leadership/201607/5-reasons-we-follow-bad-leaders.

innate need to conform to authority, recent research has found the

study participants may have acted due to followership and social

identity. "With a growing body of historical and social psychological

evidence, the present data move us toward the conclusion that agents

of brutality act as they do under the influence of a leadership with

which they are socially identified. To the extent that this identity is

salient (and competing identities are not), this provides them with their

moral compass. It also motivates them to act as followers, willing to do

what it takes to work toward the collective goals that the leader sets

out."[164]

The election of 1828 was a form of vindication for President

Andrew Jackson. In the previous election of 1824, Jackson won the

popular vote, but John Quincy Adams was elected president after

neither candidate received a majority of the vote, and the ultimate

decision of who would become president was left to the House of

Representatives. Jackson parlayed the 1824 election results into his

1828 campaign by claiming that the aristocracy of politicians allowed

---

[164] S. Reicher, S. A. Haslam, and J. Smith, "Working Toward the Experimenter," *Perspectives on Psychological Science* 7, no. 4 (2012): 315–24.

Adams to become president and the results did not reflect the political will of the ordinary Americans.

With changes in voting laws prior to this election allowing more people to vote, Jackson created a social identity for the common person by emphasizing his humble beginnings. This new social identity was inclusive and reflective of many more Americans' experiences than what was represented by Adams. [165] A common slogan used by Jackson supporters was, "Andrew Jackson and the will of the people."[166] Riding a wave of populism, Jackson easily outdistanced President Adams in 1828.

Jackson's presidential inauguration was historic if only because it showed how people who were previously nonfactors in political elections, including farmers, tradesmen, and laborers, could exert their will and their power over government. Subsequently, Jackson chose to remove experienced political stalwarts and replace them with his supporters. The strong social identity forged by President Jackson

---

[165] M. Dougherty, "Andrew Jackson Was America's 'Worst' Great President," *The Week*, February 16, 2015, accessed October 16, 2016, http://theweek.com/articles/539274/andrew-jackson-americas-worst-great-president.
[166] H. Watson, "Andrew Jackson, America's Original Anti-Establishment Candidate," *Smithsonian Magazine*, March 31, 2016, accessed March 25, 2017, http://www.smithsonianmag.com/history/andrew-jackson-americas-original-anti-establishment-candidate-180958621/.

lessened the natural checks and balances our founding fathers desired.

President Jackson tried to close the Bank of the United States (a

precursor to the Federal Reserve) and was eventually censored by the

United States Congress when he pulled all federal funds from the bank.

He also placed a number of followers in important government

positions even though they had no experience. Lastly, he forcibly

removed American Indians from land promised to them so that his

followers could claim the land.[167] When President Jackson finished his

second presidential term and headed back to his home in Tennessee,

thousands of people lined the streets to see him one last time.[168] He

had obviously struck an emotional chord among Americans and they

chose to follow President Jackson no matter how he governed.

Our choices to follow certain leaders are not always rational.

Sometimes we choose them without fully understanding how we came

to our choice. "These motivations arise from the powerful images and

[167] L. Belsie, "Five Lessons 1828 Holds for a Trump Presidency," Christian Science Monitor, November 9, 2016, accessed March 25, 2017, http://www.csmonitor.com/USA/Politics/2016/1109/Five-lessons-1828-holds-for-a-Trump-presidency.
[168] S. Ember, "Andrew Jackson Leaves Office, Martin Van Buren Becomes President," The Making of a Nation, Learning English, March 20, 2014, accessed March 25, 2017, http://learningenglish.voanews.com/a/andrew-jackson-van-buren/1775693.html.

emotions in our unconscious that we project onto our relationship with

leaders."[169] So often, you fail to realize how your emotions play a role in

your choices and that can lead to disappointment when your leaders

seem to stray from the values you have transferred to them. If people

are not drawn to or disappointed in your leadership, ask yourself if you

are creating and maintaining a shared vision that is reflective of yours

and your followers' needs.

---

[169] Maccoby, "Why People Follow The Leader."

28. President Lincoln and the Power of Empathy

Think about a time when someone openly, loudly, and in front of

people you lead told you that your decision was flat-out wrong. How did

you react in that moment? Did the hairs bristle on the back of your

neck? Did you feel your blood start to boil? How hard was it to keep

from saying something or could you even stop yourself? Would your

reaction be contingent upon the person who made such a statement?

Why do we get so emotional when we experience disagreement or

when someone tells us we are wrong?

Perceiving things and events from a singular perspective is what

your brain is programmed to do. Your eyes, ears, nose, mouth, and

sense of touch normally give you enough sensory information to make

necessary decisions. However, the brain has another area, the right

supramarginal gyrus, where compassion for others has been developed.

"This area of the brain helps us distinguish our own emotional state

from that of other people and is responsible for empathy and

compassion."[170] Because of this, you are able to recognize the emotions

---

[170] C. Bergland, "The Neuroscience of Empathy," *Psychology Today*,
October 10, 2013, accessed February 28, 2017,
https://www.psychologytoday.com/blog/the-athletes-way/201310/the-neuroscience-empathy.

other people are experiencing.

At various times in the day, your brain releases different chemicals depending on what you are doing. Endorphins are released to mask physical pain by providing pleasure, and dopamine is released to give us that feeling of satisfaction when we have accomplished something. Both of these chemicals are referred to as the me-first releases because they focus on what you are doing. Serotonin and oxytocin work in the opposite manner as they are experienced when interacting with others. Serotonin is released when you feel pride in being accepted by colleagues and loved ones while oxytocin is released when you bond with someone.[171] Since identifying trust as one of the most important factors in building an organizational culture, Dr. Paul Zak has studied the effects of oxytocin on levels of trust between people. While Zak was able to prove that the release of oxytocin reduced the fear of trusting a stranger, he also found that the release of oxytocin increased

---

[171] T. Norton, "Why the Empathetic Leader Is the Best Leader," Success, August 21, 2014, accessed February 28, 2017, http://www.success.com/article/why-the-empathetic-leader-is-the-best-leader.

empathy.[172]

President Lincoln's childhood included much suffering. He lost his

mother when he was nine and his sister when he was a teenager.

Lincoln lost many elections before eventually ascending to the

presidency. What these trials and tribulations may have done, however,

is to teach President Lincoln the value of compassion and empathy.[173]

When the Civil War began, President Lincoln always chose his

words carefully. Lincoln did not see himself as the leader of the north

armies, but rather leader of the United States. Whenever he addressed

southern states, President Lincoln often tried to empathize with

southern plantation owners as they had become reliant upon slaves

working their farms. "If slavery did not now exist amongst them, they

would not introduce it. If it did now exist amongst us, we should not

instantly give it up."[174] Even though the thought of people shackled and

---

[172] P. Zak, "The Neuroscience of Trust," *Harvard Business Review*, January–February 2017, accessed May 17, 2017, https://hbr.org/2017/01/the-neuroscience-of-trust.
[173] E. Giroux, "Lincoln's Compassion," *Massachusetts Lawyer's Weekly*, July 13, 2011, accessed February 28, 2017, http://masslawyersweekly.com/2011/07/13/lincoln%E2%80%99s-compassion/.
[174] M. Crowley, "The Leadership Genius of Abraham Lincoln," Fast Company, November 9, 2012, accessed September 8, 2016,

enslaved abhorred President Lincoln, he did his best to avoid casting

judgment while remaining firm in his belief that slavery had to be

ended. "With malice toward none, with charity for all, with firmness in

the right as God gives us to see the right, let us strive on to finish the

work we are in, to bind up the nation's wounds, to care for him who

shall have borne the battle and for his widow and his orphan, to do all

which may achieve and cherish a just and lasting peace among ourselves

and with all nations."[175]

In a study performed by the Center for Creative Leadership,

empathy was found to have a direct positive relationship with job

performance.[176] Empathy can allow you to establish deep bonds with

your followers. President Lincoln encapsulated his thoughts on empathy

with this quote, "In order to win a man to your cause, you must first

reach his heart, the great high road to his reason."[177] In order to

https://www.fastcompany.com/3002803/leadership-genius-abraham-lincoln.

[175] A. Lincoln, Lincoln's 2nd Inaugural Address, March 4, 1865, accessed February 28, 2017, http://www.bartleby.com/124/pres32.html.

[176] W. Gentry, T. Weber, and G. Sadri, *Empathy in the Workplace: A Tool for Effective Leadership* (Greensboro, NC: Center for Creative Leadership, April 2015), accessed February 28, 2017, http://www.ccl.org/wp-content/uploads/2015/04/EmpathyInTheWorkplace.pdf.

[177] Crowley, "The Leadership Genius of Abraham Lincoln."

MICHAEL BRET HOOD

negotiate the journey to reach your follower's heart, it might help if you

find a way to release oxytocin just before you get there.

29. The Backfire Effect: Why Leaders Stick to Original Opinions and Decisions despite Contradictory Evidence

Have you ever been in a meeting and heard someone present

compelling and contradictory evidence for an alternative strategy only

to see the leader remain steadfast in his or her original position? Can

you recall a time when a follower presented such evidence to you?

What if these new facts went against one of your core beliefs? Would

you look at the new information objectively or would your brain ensure

that you subjectively judged the information to align with your current

beliefs?

Confirmation bias is the process of finding information that

supports your original beliefs. The backfire effect is the reverse

dimension of confirmation bias. "So, just as confirmation bias gives us

cover to only seek out information that fits our belief system, the

backfire effect gives us cover when information blindsides us."[178]

Brendan Nyhan from the University of Michigan and Jason Reifler from

Georgia State University created fake news articles concerning hot-

---

[178] A. English, "The Social Psychology of the Backfire Effect: Locking Up the Gears of Your Mind," Homeland Security, April 29, 2016, accessed March 5, 2017, https://medium.com/homeland-security/the-social-psychology-of-the-backfire-effect-locking-up-the-gears-of-your-mind-a79d4e6e8061#.cm0j67ehz.

button issues such as weapons of mass destruction in Iraq and stem-cell

research. The fake articles were written in such a way that they served

to legitimize popular misconceptions about those topics. As soon as the

person read the fake article, they were given a truthful article detailing

in great specificity how the first article was factually incorrect.[179] Do you

think this new fact-based information changed the opinion of the

readers?

Contrary to what you may believe, the second article with the

factual information actually served as a catalyst to strengthen the

reader's initial belief. "Corrections tended to increase the strength of

people's misperceptions if those corrections contradicted their

ideologies."[180] Once you have invested in an idea, it is hard for you to

change your mind, especially if the new information conflicts with a

core belief. "Once something is added to your collections of beliefs, you

protect it from harm. You do it instinctively and unconsciously when

confronted with attitude-inconsistent information."[181]

---

[179] D. McRaney, "The Backfire Effect," You Are Not So Smart: A
Celebration of Self-Delusion, June 10, 2011, accessed March 5, 2017,
https://youarenotsosmart.com/2011/06/10/the-backfire-effect/.
[180] Ibid.
[181] Ibid.

Although you may not recognize it, your brain processes the cognitive dissonance caused by the conflicting information in a way that is favorable to your self-image. "What makes this especially worrisome is that in the process of exerting effort on dealing with cognitive dissonance produced by conflicting evidence, we actually end up building new memories and new neural connections that further strengthen our original convictions."[182] When you have deep-seated beliefs that were developed through life experiences, culture, or in-group norms, your brain silently alters facts and memories to fit them into your core beliefs.

Andrew Johnson was the vice president of the United States when President Lincoln was assassinated. Lincoln had strategically chosen Johnson to be his vice president because Johnson was believed to be a Southerner who was a supporter of the Union. In this manner, President Lincoln could offer that his presidency represented the entire United States and not just the Union states. A closer look at Johnson's history, however, revealed ulterior motives for him supporting Union ideas.

---

[182] M. Popova, "The Backfire Effect: The Psychology of Why We Have a Hard Time Changing Our Minds," Brain Pickings, May 13, 2014, accessed March 5, 2017, https://www.brainpickings.org/2014/05/13/backfire-effect-mcraney/.

Johnson grew up in a poor family, and he always harbored

resentment against Southern elites, who often owned plantations

operated with slave labor. His hatred of Southern elites led to aligning

with Union States, but that hatred didn't lead Johnson to fully adopting

the Union States' ideology. When Johnson ascended to the presidency,

his hidden beliefs about slavery became more prominent in his

decisions. Johnson was reported to have made statements such as,

"This is a country for white men and as long as I am president, it shall be

a government for white men."[183]

With such deep-rooted beliefs, President Johnson was beside

himself as Congress created bills to give civil rights to former slaves. At

every turn, President Johnson did his best to obstruct the

reconstruction efforts of Congress. For example, Johnson overturned an

order by General Sherman, which was approved by President Lincoln,

promising to redistribute land to former slaves and instead, gave the

---

[183] E. Mason, "The 5 Most Notorious Presidents in US History, History Extra," *BBC History Magazine*, November 9, 2016, accessed March 3, 2017, http://www.historyextra.com/article/feature/5-most-notorious-presidents-us-history-nixon-buchanan-jackson-harding-johnson.

land in question back to white plantation owners.[184] President Johnson also vetoed a bill to fund an agency that was helping former slaves make their way into society while also fervently fighting any effort by Congress to provide citizenship to former slaves.[185]

The more Congress did for reconstruction efforts, the more Johnson fell victim to the backfire effect. In the midterm elections of 1866, President Johnson went on a speaking tour, denouncing members of Congress for their efforts to provide rights to former slaves, with the hopes that incumbent congressmen would be defeated. Congress, in turn, created a law disallowing President Johnson to remove any cabinet member previously appointed by President Lincoln. When President Johnson violated the law, he was impeached. While waiting for and during the impeachment trial, which lasted eleven weeks, President Johnson offered olive branches to the Republican Party by promising to support future reconstruction efforts and to refrain from denouncing congressional members. President Johnson avoided an impeachment conviction by one vote only after he had agreed to

---

[184] H. L. Gates, Jr., "The Truth Behind '40 Acres And A Mule,'" PBS, accessed March 5, 2017, http://www.pbs.org/wnet/african-americans-many-rivers-to-cross/history/the-truth-behind-40-acres-and-a-mule/.
[185] Ibid.

appoint a well-liked Republican to the Secretary of War position.[186]

Cognitively, it is easier to accept what we consider to be true than to try and assimilate new information that doesn't fit into our current core of beliefs. People such as Benjamin Franklin were aware of the consequences of succumbing to the backfire effect. "In disputes upon moral or scientific points, ever let your aim be to come at truth, not to conquer your opponent. So you never shall be at a loss in losing the argument, and gaining a new discovery."[187] As a leader, would you rather make the correct decision or would you rather watch your decision backfire?

[186] Ibid.
[187] Popova, "The Backfire Effect."

30. President Jefferson, the Declaration of Independence and Criticism: Lessons for Leaders

When someone criticizes you, does it feel like you have just taken a strong punch in the gut? Do your emotions spark? Do you feel blood starting to boil? Are you ready to answer the critique with the multitude of reasons why the assessment is incorrect?

Why does criticism cause us to raise our defenses? Certainly, sometimes criticism comes with negative intentions. However, there also are times when the person providing the critique has no other motive than to try to help make you better. Are we still as hasty to dismiss these valid critiques? As leaders, should we allow criticism to hijack our senses? Why does criticism have such a profound effect upon us?

It turns out our brain reacts differently to positive and negative stimulation. Professor Richard Boyatzis and members of the Cleveland Clinic performed brain scans as people went through interviews focused on favorable goal-oriented scenarios and unfavorable problem-focused interviews. When prompted with positive suggestions, the interviewee's brain lit up in the reward center areas associated with good feelings and happy memories. When prompted with negative suggestions or

criticism, the interviewee's brain responded with anxiety and other

fearful feelings.[188]

When someone criticizes you, it is natural for you to distort the

message. You focus on the negative as if being deemed substandard in

one area means you are substandard in all. As the mind wanders

replaying the critique over and over, anxiety, anger, and other emotions

can overwhelm you. However, if you are able to focus, you can more

accurately judge the intentions of the critique. Was it truly meant to

harm you personally or was the intent to make you or the work product

better?

President Thomas Jefferson was the principal author of the

Declaration of Independence. Jefferson worked on a draft of the

Declaration for a number of days before submitting it to the Continental

Congress on June 28, 1776. Once submitted, the document underwent

extensive review from Continental Congress members. Approximately

---

[188] D. Goleman, "When You Criticize Someone, You Make It Harder for that Person to Change," *Harvard Business Review*, December 19, 2013, accessed July 2, 2016, https://hbr.org/2013/12/when-you-criticize-someone-you-make-it-harder-for-them-to-change/.

one-fifth of the draft was removed or edited.[189] As other congressional

members tightened, edited, and altered the document, Jefferson

seethed even after the Declaration of Independence was ratified on July

4, 1776. Despite the efforts of Benjamin Franklin to comfort him,

Jefferson, believing his text to be mangled, fell into a state of depression

that lasted an entire summer.[190]

President Jefferson was no different from us when it came to

accepting criticism from others. Leaders who understand how the brain

works when criticism is given or received are better prepared to deal

with the inevitable response. If you can keep from taking criticism or the

reaction to criticism personally and respond using positive language,

you can move the brain from thoughts of retaliation to potential for

growth.[191] If we, as leaders, can focus our minds when criticism is given

---

[189] "Jefferson and the Declaration," the Jefferson Monticello, accessed July 2, 2016, https://www.monticello.org/site/jefferson/jefferson-and-declaration.

[190] L. Lehrman, "Jefferson May Have Drafted the Declaration of Independence, but He Wasn't Happy Being Edited," *Fox News Opinion*, July 2, 2010, accessed July 2, 2016, http://www.foxnews.com/opinion/2010/06/30/lewis-lehrman-editing-declaration-independence-jefferson-franklin-congress.html.

[191] M. Thomas, "Six Reasons Why Criticism Is a Good Thing," *The Guardian*, February 9, 2012, July 2, 2016, https://www.theguardian.com/culture-professionals-network/culture-professionals-blog/2012/feb/09/reasons-tips-criticism-arts.

or received, we just might be able to learn something about ourselves

as well as our followers.

31. President Obama's Fight against Decision Fatigue

How many times have you yawned while at work? Maybe you didn't get enough sleep the night before or maybe you've just been working too hard, but have you stopped to think how fatigue can affect your leadership? Do you think your brain works at its optimal best when you are tired? Is it possible or even likely that fatigue has an impact on your decision-making ability? Lastly, do you think the time of day has any impact on your decisions or your decision-making process?

Daniel Kahneman wrote a groundbreaking book called *Thinking, Fast and Slow,* where he discussed the brain's decision-making processes by classifying them into two distinct systems. System 1 is referred to as the reactionary brain characterized by choices made without using the reasoning process.[192] An example of System 1 is when an unexpected person, object, or animal darts in front of your car and you automatically slam on your brakes without thinking about it. The System 2 brain operates on reason and logic.[193] An example of System 2 is when you purchase a car and have considered the options you want, the type of car you want, and the price you are willing to pay. If you had

---

[192] D. Kahneman, *Thinking, Fast and Slow* (New York: Farrar, Straus and Giroux, 2011).
[193] Ibid.

to guess, which system do you spend most of your day in, System 1 or System 2?

You may be surprised to know that most of your daily decisions are made using System 1. These reactionary behaviors are based on stereotypes that are derived from your culture, your upbringing, your life experiences, and even your friends and peers. You may like to believe that you have rationally thought out your choices by using System 2, but more often than not, System 1 has subconsciously made the choice for you. Fatigue causes you to rely even further on System 1 even though you may not realize it. Decision fatigue, which is referred to as the gradual erosion of effective decision-making ability caused by the need to focus on earlier decisions, is a problem that besets many leaders. "The more choices you make throughout the day, the harder each one becomes for your brain, and eventually it looks for shortcuts."[194] These shortcuts can lead to impulsivity or decision avoidance. Both outcomes represent potential danger for leaders.

Every US president has been faced with tough decisions, but as

---

[194] J. Tierney, "Do You Suffer from Decision Fatigue?," *New York Times*, August 17, 2011, accessed October 25, 2016, http://www.nytimes.com/2011/08/21/magazine/do-you-suffer-from-decision-fatigue.html?_r=0.

the world grows smaller and with technology playing a part in

everything we do, making decisions has never been more complicated.

President Barack Obama realized that he could easily succumb to

decision fatigues due to the amount of information available as well as

the number of decisions he needed to make every day. As a leader, he

wanted to make the best decisions possible, so he took steps to protect

himself from decision fatigue.

If you needed President Obama to make a decision about

something before you could go forward, you were required to submit a

decision memo outlining the facts of the matter at hand. In addition,

President Obama, in an effort to streamline his decision-making

process, would require you to include three boxes at the bottom of each

request titled, "Agree," "Disagree," and "Let's discuss." By approaching

decision making in this manner, President Obama limited the potential

effects of decision fatigue.[195] If he could quickly agree or disagree to a

proposed decision, he did not have to mentally focus on the idea past

the initial reading. When the "Let's Discuss" box was checked, President

Obama was essentially carving out time in the future where he could

---

[195] S. Blanda, How Barack Obama Gets Things Done, 99U, 2013, accessed
October 9, 2016, http://99u.com/articles/7223/how-barack-obama-
gets-things-done.

focus on the proposal with other advisors and attempt to make a better decision.

What is dangerous about decision fatigue is that you, as a leader, do not always recognize its presence. Jonathan Levav of Stanford University and Shai Danziger of Ben-Gurion University studied decision fatigue in relation to judicial decisions made at different times of the day. "Prisoners who appeared early in the morning received parole about 70% of the time, while those who appeared late in the day were paroled less than 10% of the time."[196] After making decision after decision, these judges suffered from fatigue, and in many cases, unconsciously chose the safest option, which was returning the prisoner to jail.

Inasmuch as System 2 works like a cell-phone battery, reducing the number of things you have to focus on or even taking small respites in your day can help to recharge your System 2 batteries, which will subsequently increase the probability of you making more rational decisions. The next time you find yourself mentally exhausted, take a step away, get yourself something to eat, or find a way to get some

---

[196] Tierney, "Do You Suffer From Decision Fatigue?"

exercise. Doing so may just save you from a decision you later come to

regret.

32. Resilience in Leadership: Contrasting the Aftermath of the 2016 Presidential Election with President Bush's 9/11 Response

Have you ever had a major setback in your personal or professional life? How did the setback impact your mind-set? Did it cause you to fall into a tailspin or did it make you more committed to achieving success? Would your response to the setback be different if you were the leader? How important is a leader's response to followers when both suffer a significant defeat, misfortune, or difficulty?

Martin Seligman, the director of the Positive Psychology Center at the University of Pennsylvania, has studied failure and helplessness for years before he pivoted to resilience after discovering "learned helplessness." Seligman and Donald Hiroto came up with an experiment where they separated volunteers into three different groups, with one group being able to press a button to turn off a loud and annoying noise, one group unable to hear the same noise, and the last group unable to turn off the noise no matter what they did. The very next day, the groups were brought back and all were subjected to a similar loud and annoying noise. In order to remove the noise, all the participants had to do was move their hands approximately twelve inches. The group who didn't hear the noise and the group that was able to turn the

noise off by pressing a button quickly figured out how to eliminate the

problem. Most members of the group forced to endure the noise the

previous day made no attempt to stop it.

Despite being completely helpless in the previous day's

experiment, there were always approximately one-third of group

members who didn't succumb to their previous experience. Rather,

they continued working until they figured out how to turn the noise

off.[197] Why are some people resilient in the face of setbacks and defeat

when others are not?

Facing a setback, loss, or a feeling of helplessness is difficult. Yet,

an important tenet of leadership is the ability to bounce back and show

resilience in the face of difficulty. "It requires the courage to confront

painful realities, the faith that there will be a solution when one isn't

immediately evident, and the tenacity to carry on despite a nagging gut

---

[197] M. Seligman, "Building Resilience," *Harvard Business Review*, April 2011, accessed November 10, 2016, https://hbr.org/2011/04/building-resilience.

feeling that the situation is hopeless." [198] It appears that much of

resilience depends on how you frame the question. "Frame adversity as

a challenge, and you become more flexible and able to deal with it,

move on, learn from it, and grow. Focus on it, frame it as a threat, and a

potentially traumatic event becomes an enduring problem; you become

more inflexible, and more likely to be negatively affected."[199]

After the 2016 US presidential votes were tallied and Donald

Trump was declared the president-elect, a number of colleges and

universities canceled classes, exams, and meetings because of the

election results. The reasons were varied, but they all had to do with the

unexpected victory by Trump. "People are frustrated, people are just

really sad and shocked," said Trey Boynton, the director of multi-ethnic

student affairs at the University of Michigan. "A lot of people are feeling

like there has been a loss. We talked about grief today and the loss of

hope that this election would solidify the progress that was being

made." Some of the upset students retreated into Ms. Boynton's office

[198] S. Snyder, "Why Is Resilience So Hard," *Harvard Business Review*, November 6, 2013, accessed November 10, 2016, https://hbr.org/2013/11/why-is-resilience-so-hard.
[199] M. Konnikova, "How People Learn to Become Resilient," *The New Yorker*, February 11, 2016, accessed November 10, 2016, http://www.newyorker.com/science/maria-konnikova/the-secret-formula-for-resilience.

to color in coloring books and play with Play-Doh in order to help them forget about the election results.[200]

Contrast their behavior with the events of September 11, 2001. People from all over the world were in shock. Lives were lost. People were scared. Adversity permeated everyone's conscious, and many people looked to President George W. Bush for leadership. If there ever was a situation that called for resilience, the events of 9/11 were it.

From the outset, President Bush made it clear that he possessed the resilience required of an event like 9/11. "The pictures of airplanes flying into buildings, fires burning, huge—huge structures collapsing have filled us with disbelief, terrible sadness and a quiet unyielding anger. These acts of mass murder were intended to frighten our nation into chaos and retreat. But they have failed. Our country is strong. A great people has been moved to defend a great nation."[201] If President

---

[200] M. Korn and D. Belkin, "Colleges Try to Comfort Students Upset by Trump Victory," *Wall Street Journal*, November 9, 2016, accessed November 10, 2016, http://blogs.wsj.com/washwire/2016/11/09/colleges-try-to-comfort-students-upset-by-trump-victory/.
[201] P. Ross, "9/11 Anniversary 2014: 25 Quotes and Moments from Sept. 11th, 2001 and after," *International Business Times*, September 11, 2014, accessed November 10, 2016, http://www.ibtimes.com/911-anniversary-2014-25-quotes-moments-sept-11-2001-after-1684296.

Bush had not shown resilience in this moment, what would have happened to the United States?

The good news is resilience can be learned. Numerous studies have shown that how we look at events can determine whether or not we will be able to overcome the adversity we face. "Seligman found that training people to change their explanatory styles from internal to external ("Bad events aren't my fault"), from global to specific ("This is one narrow thing rather than a massive indication that something is wrong with my life"), and from permanent to impermanent ("I can change the situation, rather than assuming it's fixed") made them more psychologically successful and less prone to depression."[202] How we look at our defeats and challenges can dictate our responses.

As a leader, you are going to face adversity whether you like it or not. How you respond in these moments will have a significant impact on your leadership credibility. When that moment comes, will you fall into a downward spiral unable to face or accept that things did not go as you had hoped, or will you be resilient and work to overcome your adverse moments?

---

[202] Konnikova, "How People Learn To Become Resilient."

33. Fading to Gray: How Ethical Fading Impacted President Reagan

How important is ethical behavior to a leader or a follower? Could you effectively lead a group of people if you engaged in unethical behavior? Likewise, could you follow someone who you perceived to have committed a major ethical infraction? How would you respond if you were asked to rate your own ability to make ethical decisions?

For many people, the idea of ethics is simple. There is right, and there is wrong. For some people, though, there is an expansive gray area where right and wrong may not be so clear. Yet there are many occasions where leaders clearly take unethical actions. How can someone who you would consider to be ethical make a decision or take an action that is so clearly unethical?

Ann Tenbrunsel and David Messick have been studying a concept they termed "ethical fading," the process by which clear ethical decisions somehow fade into a gray area, allowing the decision maker to forego their ethical self-concept and make an unethical choice.[203] Our

---

[203] A. Tenbrunsel and D. Messick, "Ethical Fading: The Role of Self-Deception in Unethical Behavior," *Social Justice Research* 17, no. 2 (2004): 223–36, accessed February 26, 2017,

natural penchant for self-deception is a prime motivator for ethical

fading. "By avoiding or disguising the moral implications of a decision,

individuals can behave in a self-interested manner and still hold the

conviction they are ethical persons."[204]

Tenbrunsel and Messick have identified certain enablers that allow

you to engage in self-deception so that your unethical choices fit within

your perceived ethical profile. One such enabler is language

euphemisms.[205] When you refer to using another employee to

accomplish a personal goal as "collateral damage," you are engaging in

self-deception in order to preserve your favorable and ethical self-

image. Another means to ethical fading is through repetition of

unethical behavior, which makes it easier for you to repeat unethical

behaviors after engaging in them initially.[206]

There is also a concept called advantageous comparison in which

you would frame your decision in such a way that it mitigates your

unethical action. How many times have you justified one of your

https://business.illinois.edu/files/responsibility/docs/ethical-fading-2004.pdf.
[204] Ibid.
[205] Ibid.
[206] Ibid.

decisions by saying, "Yes, but they did this?" This kind of framing can

also lead to the devaluation of the victim. Justification occurs quickly

when you rationalize your behavior by reasoning that whoever was

affected by your unethical decision deserved such action.[207]

President Reagan was a vocal enemy of communism. During his

term as president, Nicaragua's government was in turmoil as Cuban

backed communist Sandinistas were fighting with Contras for control of

the country. President Reagan sought to assist the Contras, but the

Democratic Congress wasn't as enthusiastic about the cause as was

President Reagan. In 1984, Congress passed the Boland Amendment,

which made financial or military aid to the Nicaraguan Contras legally

impossible.[208]

President Reagan was once quoted as saying, "Freedom prospers

when religion is vibrant and the rule of law under God is

---

[207] R. Riggio, "The Science of Why Good People Do Bad Things," *Psychology Today*, November 1, 2014, accessed February 26, 2017, https://www.psychologytoday.com/blog/cutting-edge-leadership/201411/the-science-why-good-people-do-bad-things.
[208] "The Iran-Contra Affair," PBS, accessed February 26, 2017, http://www.pbs.org/wgbh/americanexperience/features/general-article/reagan-iran/.

acknowledged."[209] Despite his praise for the rule of law, President

Reagan, after Congress passed the Boland Amendment, told his national

security advisor, Robert McFarlane, to do whatever it took to keep the

Contras in operation.[210]

At about the same time, the government of Iran secretly

approached the United States to ascertain if the United States would be

willing to sell arms to Iran in order for them to fight against the

government of Iraq. President Reagan began the process of ethical

fading by convincing himself that his agreement to sale of arms to Iran,

in part, was a means to fund the fight against communism. After the

arms deal became public, US attorney general Edwin Meese found that

only $12 million out of $30 million in payments from Iran could be

traced. Lieutenant Colonel Oliver North eventually testified that the

missing $18 million was diverted to the Nicaraguan Contras with the

implicit understanding that President Reagan had approved of the

siphoning of funds. The Tower Commission eventually determined that

---

[209] R. Reagan, "Excerpts from President's Speech to Association of Evangelicals," *The New York Times*, March 9, 1983, accessed February 26, 2017, http://www.nytimes.com/1983/03/09/us/excerpts-from-president-s-speech-to-national-association-of-evangelicals.html?pagewanted=all.
[210] "The Iran-Contra Affair."

President Reagan's "disengaged" leadership allowed these illegal transfers to occur.[211]

When President Reagan referred to the Soviet Union as "the focus of evil in the modern world," his process of ethical fading had begun.[212] The euphemism became a repetitive reference as well as an iconic devaluation of an enemy. With the battle framed as good versus evil, President Reagan, whether he knew it or not, was creating an advantageous comparison from which his followers could easily engage in self-deception. Therefore, diverting funds to the Contras in spite of the Boland Amendment specifications became an act of heroism instead of a violation of law. In his opening statement to the joint Iran-Contra Congressional Committee, Lieutenant Colonel Oliver North said, "I observed the president to be a leader who cared deeply about people and who believed that the interests of our country were advanced by recognizing that ours is a nation at risk in a dangerous world, and acting accordingly."[213]

---

[211] Ibid.

[212] Reagan, "Excerpts from President's Speech to Association of Evangelicals."

[213] O. North, "Opening Statement to the Joint Iran-Contra Congressional Committee," American Rhetoric, July 9, 1987, accessed February 26,

Self-deception is one of those natural processes that allow us to

see ourselves in a favorable manner even when we choose to act

unethically. This is why so many studies have revealed that we are not

nearly as ethical as we perceive ourselves to be. President Reagan

recognized his self-deception when he said, "I let my preoccupation

with the hostages intrude into areas it didn't belong. The image – the

reality – of Americans in chains deprived of their freedom and their

families so far from home, burdened my thoughts. And this was a

mistake." [214] Leaders who understand how framing questions,

circumstances, and facts can lead to unethical behavior are better

prepared to overcome these natural tendencies. You probably have the

best of intentions as a leader, but if you're not careful, things that are

clearly black and white ethically can fade to gray. If you allow these

ethical boundaries to fade, will that affect your leadership ability?

2017,
http://www.americanrhetoric.com/speeches/olivernorthfrancontrahear
ing.htm.
[214] Reagan, R. (1987). Address to the Nation on the Iran Arms and
Contra Aid Controversy and Administration Goals, August 12, 1987.
Accessed October 8, 2017
http://www.presidency.ucsb.edu/ws/index.php?pid=34693

34. Because I Said So: How President Kennedy Fell into the Consistency Trap

Have you ever reluctantly made a promise to someone and

immediately wished you hadn't committed to such a thing? As you

experienced regret, did you think about backing out of the promise?

Chances are, you stuck with your promise and followed through even

though you didn't want to. Why do you think you did that?

Consistency is a hallmark of the human psyche. Once you say

you are going to do something or once you express your opinion,

especially if you do it publicly, you will be very reluctant to go against

your words. Consistency of actions and words is directly related to your

self-image. If you do not carry through your commitments, you allow

the inaction to negatively impact your confidence.[215]

The psychology of the commitment can be a powerful tool for you

as a leader. A leader once shared a story about three employees, who

despite his efforts, refused to collaborate with each other causing

duplicity. Each employee agreed to pursue collaboration when asked in

---

[215] R. Cialdini, *Influence: The Psychology of Persuasion*, rev. ed.; 1st
Collins business essentials ed. (New York: Collins, 2007).

private conversations, yet it was only when the leader brought all three

employees together in a room and had them publicly commit to

collaboration did the leader see the change he desired.

While our need for consistency can be a tool to use, it can also be a

potentially serious problem. In a study done by Norbert L. Kerr and

Robert J. MacCoun, participants, acting in the capacity of a jury, were

more likely to be a hung jury (one which could not unanimously agree) if

jurors were polled in a voice vote as opposed to secret ballot.[216] By

making their opinions public, it was harder for the study participants to

go against their initial declarations, even if the competing parties made

compelling arguments.

When the Kennedy administration learned that the Soviet

Union had placed nuclear missiles on the island of Cuba, President

Kennedy publicly announced that the United States of America would

not allow that to continue. Thirteen days of tense gamesmanship and

negotiation followed. Finally, the Soviet Union agreed to remove the

missiles from Cuba. President Kennedy's public outrage delivered the

---

[216] N. Kerr and R. MacCoun, "The Effects of Jury Size and Polling Method on the Process and Product of Jury Deliberation," *Journal of Personality and Social Psychology* 48 (1985): 349–63.

message that the United States would not stand for actions counter to

their interests, especially in a location so close to its land.

Since that time, however, more has been learned about the

crisis including secret tapes that were made by President Kennedy.

Historians who listened to these tapes learned a vastly different version

of events that were not given to the public at the time they occurred.

The Soviet Union brought the missiles to Cuba because the United

States had placed similar missiles in Turkey. There were plenty of

discussions in Kennedy's cabinet about how to lead in this situation, but

most advisors agreed that having missiles pointed at the United States

in Cuba was no different than having missiles pointed at the United

States in the Soviet Union. Based on the models, the strikes, no matter

where they originated, would arrive at about the same time. The

difference was that President Kennedy had made a public commitment

to have the Soviet Union remove the Cuban missiles. By uttering such a

statement aloud and in the press, President Kennedy fell victim to the

consistency trap where he psychologically faced a need to follow

through, even though the statement took the United States and the

Soviet Union to the brink of a nuclear war.

To his credit, President Kennedy worked tirelessly behind the scenes and led in a mature manner. Despite some of his cabinet members wanting to take a more hawkish view, President Kennedy quietly negotiated an agreement with Soviet leader Khrushchev, wherein the Soviet Union would remove their missiles from Cuba and the United States would remove their missiles from Turkey. Only a few members of President Kennedy's team knew about this agreement, because Kennedy wanted people to believe that he followed through on his commitment.[217]

If you are to be a successful leader, you must understand the power of the consistency theory as well as how it applies to you and your followers. Understanding how this decision-making trap affects you can help mitigate the unconscious need to follow through when you have made an incorrect decision. Would your followers want you to follow through on something just because you said it or would they prefer a leader who was willing to admit an error and self-correct before any real damage was done?

---

[217] B. Schwarz, "The Real Cuban Missile Crisis," *The Atlantic*, January/February 2013, accessed August 15, 2016, http://www.theatlantic.com/magazine/archive/2013/01/the-real-cuban-missile-crisis/309190/.

35. Everyone Is Watching: The Importance of Self-Regulation in Emotional Intelligence

Has there ever been an instance where you felt like you earned a promotion only to see it go to some other person in your organization? How did you feel when you didn't get the position? Were you angry? Disappointed? Did your leadership or performance suffer after this rejection?

If you think that rejection doesn't affect your mood, you might be surprised to learn that rejection activates the same areas of the brain as when we experience physical pain.[218] Rejection, despite the brain's response, is an emotional pain that damages our self-esteem. This, in turn, initiates anger as well as a fight or flight response. In order to reestablish self-esteem, it would not be abnormal for you to seek direct compliance from followers by issuing orders or decrees in order to reestablish your self-confidence. If positional power is lost through the rejection, the messenger or person who embodies the rejection can be seen as the culprit, and you will have a hard time forgiving that person.

---

[218] G. Winch, "10 Surprising Facts About Rejection," *Psychology Today*, July 3, 2013, accessed August 7, 2016, https://www.psychologytoday.com/blog/the-squeaky-wheel/201307/10-surprising-facts-about-rejection.

Experiencing such a situation can have negative effects on your followers because of something called mirror neurons. "Mirror neurons have particular importance in organizations because leaders' emotions and actions prompt followers to mirror those feelings and deeds."[219] If you hold on to your anger, do not be surprised when your followers reciprocate your behavior.

President John Adams sought reelection in 1800, but his opponent was Thomas Jefferson, a formidable and well-known candidate. Prior to this election, both Jefferson and Adams had worked together on many projects to include drafting the United States Constitution. However, in the bitterly contested election, Jefferson's supporters referred to President Adams as "hideous and hermaphroditical" while President Adams's supporters referred to Jefferson as "mean-spirited and low-lived."[220] When Jefferson defeated Adams in the election limiting Adams to a single presidential term, President Adams was so upset he refused

---

[219] Goleman and Boyatzis, "Social Intelligence and the Biology of Leadership," 1–9.
[220] K. Calamur, "A Short History of Awkward Presidential Transitions," *The Atlantic*, November 10, 2016, accessed March 25, 2017, https://www.theatlantic.com/politics/archive/2016/11/presidential-transition-obama-trump/507257/.

to attend President Jefferson's inauguration.[221]

In 1802, the *Richmond Recorder* published a story reporting that President Jefferson had a black slave mistress who had borne him children. The ensuing scandal rocked the new nation. President Jefferson never denied the accusation like some of his supporters expected. At least one Presidential scholar now believes that it may have been President Adams who leaked the information for the story. At the time, the two men remained bitter enemies. [222] It wasn't until Benjamin Rush, a Declaration signer and mutual friend of Presidents Adams and Jefferson, reported cordial comments made by President Adams about President Jefferson did the relationship renew.[223] Despite the amicable reunion, President Adams was never able to undo his actions and correct the snub of his friend.

---

[221] "Adams Friend (And Rival), America's Story," Library of Congress, accessed August 4, 2016, http://www.americaslibrary.gov/aa/adams/aa_adams_jefferson_3.html .

[222] M. Silk, "Did John Adams Out Thomas Jefferson and Sally Hemings," *Smithsonian Magazine*, November 2016, accessed March 25, 2017, http://www.smithsonianmag.com/history/john-adams-out-thomas-jefferson-sally-hemings-180960789/.

[223] Unknown Author(s). John Adams, The Thomas Jefferson Foundation. Accessed October 8, 2017 https://www.monticello.org/site/jefferson/john-adams

When your emotions take over, you respond accordingly.

Sometimes this leads you to do things you later regret. The difference

for leaders is that when you allow your emotional hijackings to occur,

your followers are watching to see the example you are setting, and

because of mirror neurons, they are more likely to replicate your

behavior. You will never be perfect, but as President Adams has shown,

you can't always go back and fix what you should have done in the first

place...especially when everyone is watching.

36. Psychopathy, Leadership, and US Presidents

What are the leadership traits of top US presidents? Would you be surprised if surveys indicated that the most well-respected presidents lead with fearlessness? Would the best US presidents have the ability to strongly influence others? Do you think these presidents allow stress to interfere with leading? What would you say if the traits listed above were also linked to psychopaths?

The Psychopath Personality Inventory (PPI-R) is an accepted, standardized assessment of psychopathic traits in individuals. There are eight component traits in the test and the first three traits, social influence, fearlessness, and stress immunity, are also referred to as the fearless dominance traits.[224] If a person scores high in these trait areas, it does not necessarily mean he or she is a psychopath, but it reveals that this person has certain traits in common with psychopaths.

Researchers went to various biographers, journalists, historians, and political scholars to calculate the PPI-R scores for past US presidents (up to President George W. Bush). The US president who scored highest

---

[224] C. Wallis, "Of Psychopaths and Presidential Candidates," *Scientific American*, August 12, 2016, accessed October 8, 2016, https://blogs.scientificamerican.com/mind-guest-blog/of-psychopaths-and-presidential-candidates/.

in the fearless dominance traits was Teddy Roosevelt, followed by John

F. Kennedy, Franklin D. Roosevelt, Ronald Reagan, Rutherford B. Hayes,

Zachary Taylor, Bill Clinton, Martin Van Buren, Andrew Jackson, and

George W. Bush.[225]

Surprisingly, these traits had a positive correlation in the areas

of presidential performance, leadership, persuasiveness, crisis

management, and congressional relations.[226] Having these

psychopathic-related traits can also lead to other less desired behaviors.

"Certain psychopathic traits may be like a double-edged sword. Fearless

dominance, for example, may contribute to reckless criminality and

violence."[227] In addition, people who score high in the fearless

dominance domain traits can often be sexual predators and rarely, if at

all, pay attention to risk.

---

[225] J. Howard, "Psychopathic Personality Traits Linked with Presidential Success, Psychologists Suggest," *Huffington Post*, September 13, 2012, accessed October 8, 2016, http://www.huffingtonpost.com/2012/09/13/psychopathic-personality-traits-president_n_1874567.html.
[226] D. DiSalvo, "What Makes Presidents and Psychopaths Similar?," *Forbes*, September 15, 2012, accessed October 8, 2016, http://www.forbes.com/sites/daviddisalvo/2012/09/15/what-makes-presidents-and-psychopaths-similar/#20e1abee2d97.
[227] Howard, Psychopathic Personality Traits Linked with Presidential Success, Psychologists Suggest."

On October 14, 1912, President Teddy Roosevelt was ready to deliver a speech in Milwaukee. On his way to the podium, a disgruntled citizen shot President Roosevelt. Instead of seeking medical assistance, President Roosevelt continued onto the podium and delivered his speech. In the speech, President Roosevelt told the audience, "I don't know whether you fully understand that I have just been shot; but it takes more than that to kill a Bull Moose."[228] President Roosevelt continued with his speech by telling the audience, "The bullet is in me now, so that I cannot make a very long speech, but I will try my best."[229] In this instance, the traits of fearless dominance are present. President Roosevelt, after being shot, showed little regard for stress, practiced a form of interpersonal dominance by proudly refusing to cede the stage, and exhibited utter fearlessness in the face of the bold assassination attempt.

Yet fearless dominance traits can also lead presidents to questionable decisions. When President Bill Clinton had a sexual affair with White House intern Monica Lewinsky, he was showing the negative side of the fearless dominance traits. The idea of stress and anxiety over

---

[228] DiSalvo, "What Makes Presidents and Psychopaths Similar?"
[229] Ibid.

what might happen if he entered such an affair did not impact him like it would for individuals who score lower in the fearless dominance domains. "It's not that they can't feel fear or anxiety, but it takes a much more extreme situation to elicit these emotions." People with the fearless dominance traits thrive on the adulation of others and they live for the thrill involved with risk.[230]

The psychopathic fearless dominance traits, whether you know it or not, affect your perceptions of leaders. In some cases, these traits can help your leader excel, such as in times of crisis, while in other situations, these traits will cause your leader to succumb to deceitful and self-serving behavior.

You are also likely to possess certain levels of the fearless dominance traits as part of your character. As a leader, will you leverage those traits to improve your performance when your followers most need you, or will you allow those traits to corrupt your credibility and send your leadership crashing in a downward spiral?

---

[230] M. Prigg, "The Secret of Their Success? How U.S. Leaders from JFK to Teddy Roosevelt to George W Bush Share Character Traits with Psychopaths," *The Daily Mail*, September 12, 2012, accessed October 8, 2016, http://www.dailymail.co.uk/sciencetech/article-2202013/Are-presidents-psychopaths-How-U-S-leaders-JFK-Roosevelt-George-W-Bush-fearless-dominant.html.

37. President Polk, the Workaholic

Have you ever worked for a leader who lived and breathed

everything work? Did you notice that every conversation, no matter

how it started, ended up with a discussion involving the workplace? Can

an obsession with work cause harm to both your mind and body? How

does being a workaholic affect your leadership?

Americans are notorious workaholics. In a *60 Minutes/Vanity Fair*

survey, more than half of the respondents said that monitoring e-mails

outside of work hours was routine.[231] The manifestations of being a

workaholic results in not taking vacation time, an unhealthy work-life

balance, and an increased risk of suicide. An amazing three-quarters of

the American workforce does not use all of their vacation time

according to a Glassdoor survey.[232] This can have a deleterious effect

on your organizational efficiency and productivity. Employees who elect

to take time off of work are 82 percent more productive when they

---

[231] P. Reaney, "Americans Are Definitely Workaholics," Business Insider
via Reuters, July 8, 2015, accessed February 17, 2017,
http://uk.businessinsider.com/r-checking-work-emails-at-home-its-part-
of-the-job-for-most-americans-2015-7?r=US&IR=T.
[232] B. Covert, "Taking a Vacation May Save Your Career," New Republic,
June 23, 2014, accessed February 17, 2017,
https://newrepublic.com/article/118285/workaholism-america-hurting-
economy.

return from vacation.[233] This is why some organizations make taking a

certain amount of vacation time mandatory.

Besides the psychological risks of working too much, there are also

physiological ramifications. Workaholics have higher levels of

adrenaline, which over time, lead to increased cholesterol levels,

narrowing of the capillaries that supply blood to the heart, a decrease in

the body's ability to remove cholesterol, higher levels of plaque

deposits, and increased blood clotting.[234] Working too much also affects

sleep patterns. When you don't get at least seven hours of sleep every

night, you have a much harder time concentrating.[235] Working too much

for too long can lead to severe exhaustion as well as strong feelings of

depression and in some cases even death.[236]

President James Polk was an admitted workaholic. In his 1848

address to Congress, President Polk said, "No president who performs

his duties faithfully and conscientiously can have any leisure." Historical

---

[233] Ibid.
[234] B. Killinger, "The Workaholic Breakdown—The Loss of Health," *Psychology Today*, April 30, 2013, accessed February 17, 2017, https://www.psychologytoday.com/blog/the-workaholics/201304/the-workaholic-breakdown-the-loss-health.
[235] Covert, "Taking a Vacation May Save Your Career."
[236] Killinger, "The Workaholic Breakdown."

records show that President Polk left Washington, DC, for overnight

trips on only four occasions during his single term as US president, and

even some of those trips were work related. The first lady even tried to

intervene at times by planning social gatherings at the White House. In

these instances, President Polk would attend the function but make

sure that he woke up extra early the next morning so that he could

make up for lost work time that was spent at the party.[237] Polk died only

three months after his presidential term ended.

The Japanese refer to "karoshi" as death from work.[238] With

smartphones and technology, it seems to be harder and harder to

separate from work. You may or may not understand the damage you

are doing to your body, but are you also considering the potential

damage you are doing to your followers? As a leader, your actions and

behaviors are contagious. Are you setting the right example for your

followers?

---

[237] Brandus, *Under This Roof.*
[238] Killinger, "The Workaholic Breakdown."

38. President Jefferson, Vision, and the Louisiana Purchase

Have you ever experienced a leader who had crazy ideas? Were there people in your organization who loudly or silently ridiculed the leader's vision? Did their harmful words have any kind of negative impact on your visionary leader or did he or she work that much harder to attain the goal? Do you have a vision of the future that is forward looking and responsive to the needs of your followers?

So many times in history, leaders have dreamed of a different future than what most people can see. Sometimes, their vision seems outlandish while other times you might wonder why you had never thought of such a thing. When these leaders first speak of their new ideas, how quickly are these ideas rejected. Yet, these leaders have an important trait to keep their vision alive. "When it comes to living out a vision, persistence matters just as much as inspiration."[239]

If you have ever created a vision for your organization, chances are you recruited others to help you accomplish your vision. In order to

---

[239] J. Ryan, "Leadership Success Always Starts with Vision," *Forbes*, July 29, 2009, accessed February 28, 2017, https://www.forbes.com/2009/07/29/personal-success-vision-leadership-managing-ccl.html.

do so, you probably had to inspire your followers by establishing shared goals. "Constituents want visions of the future that reflect their own aspirations. They want to hear how their own dreams will come true and their hopes will be fulfilled."[240] Communicating these ideas, however, can be easier said than done.

With France owning the area known as Louisiana, President Jefferson foresaw the potential for conflict. The French, if they were able to control the Mississippi River, would have strategic tactical advantages against the United States if it became necessary for the country to expand. Before any potential conflict arose, President Jefferson dispatched James Monroe and Robert Livingston to determine Napoleon Bonaparte's willingness to sell the territory to the United States.

To everyone's surprise, Bonaparte welcomed the overture and offered to sell a much larger expanse of land to the United States. The initial asking price given by Napoleon was $23 million, but Monroe and Livingston negotiated the amount to $15 million, which was significantly

---

[240] J. Kouzes and B. Posner, "To Lead, Create a Shared Vision," *Harvard Business Review*, January 2009, accessed February 28, 2017, https://hbr.org/2009/01/to-lead-create-a-shared-vision.

more than what they were authorized to spend. President Jefferson

immediately faced a conundrum concerning the legality of any

agreement with Bonaparte and France. Per President Jefferson's

interpretation of the United States Constitution, the document did not

expressly permit the president to acquire territory. Jefferson initially

thought that he would need a constitutional amendment to grant him

the power to honor the purchase, but despite his personal reservations,

he also made it very clear that the United States would follow through

with the purchase. "In the meantime we must ratify and pay our money,

as we have treated, for a thing beyond the Constitution, and rely on the

nation to sanction an act done for its great good, without its previous

authority."[241] Although there were some Federalists who felt America

already had too much land and not enough money, the Louisiana

Purchase treaty was ratified on October 20, 1803, and became one of

the most important transactions in American history.[242]

[241] S. Bomboy, "The Louisiana Purchase: Jefferson's Constitutional Gamble," *Constitution Daily*, National Constitution Center, October 20, 2016, accessed February 28, 2017, http://blog.constitutioncenter.org/2016/10/the-louisiana-purchase-jeffersons-constitutional-gamble/.
[242] J. Greenspan, "8 Things You May Not Know about the Louisiana Purchase," History Channel, A & E Network, April 30, 2013, accessed

Behind the trait of honesty, looking forward is the most desired attribute of leaders.[243] In order for you to achieve buy-in from your followers, you need to connect and communicate so that followers not only see the importance of achieving these goals but also understand how this will impact their lives as well as their future. "As counterintuitive as it may seem, the best way to lead people into the future is to connect with them deeply in the present."[244] At the time of the Louisiana Purchase, President Jefferson saw a vision of America that extended from the Atlantic Ocean to the Pacific. His persistence and ability to create a shared vision among his followers led to the United States that exists today. Are you currently bonding with your followers in order to create a shared vision of the future?

February 28, 2017, http://www.history.com/news/8-things-you-may-not-know-about-the-louisiana-purchase.
[243] Kouzes and Posner, "To Lead, Create a Shared Vision."
[244] Ibid.

39. Prohibition and Psychological Reactance

How would you respond if your leader took away one of the things that you felt was an important part of your identity or your job? Would you fight your leader to get that task/role/responsibility/benefit back? Are there certain things that you believe to be so important that you cannot imagine yourself not doing them? How important are these items to your sense of self?

Jack Brehm fist coined the term "psychological reactance" in 1966 to describe the motivation to regain a freedom once it has been threatened or lost.[245] Followers have expectations of both their leader as well as their jobs. With so many people relying on their job for a significant portion of their personal identity, a leader's effort to improve efficiency, challenge followers, or innovate can easily be misinterpreted causing followers to suffer psychological reactance.

When someone suffers psychological reactance, physiological changes occur in their body. "When confronted with an illegitimate

---

[245] C. Steindl, E. Jonas, S. Sittenthaler, E. Trautt-Mattausch, and J. Greenberg, "Understanding Psychological Reactance: New Developments and Findings," *Zeitschrift für Psychologie* 223, no. 4 (2015): 205–14, accessed March 6, 2017, http://psycnet.apa.org/journals/zfp/223/4/205.pdf.

restriction, people's heart rate increased immediately."[246] Anger is often

associated with psychological reactance. "The extent to which people

are affected by threats to their freedom and the resulting motivation to

restore their freedom strongly depend on a person's self being involved

in the reactive process."[247] When something considered important is

being taken away from your follower, you are altering a part of their

identity. The more attached to the core identity, the more vehemently

they will fight to restore their sense of self.

When prohibition became law in January, 1920, alcohol was

considered to be a very serious social problem causing, among other

things, poverty, child labor, crime, and prostitution.[248] President Herbert

Hoover gave his inaugural address on March 4, 1929, and outlined what

he felt were the problems facing America. "With sweeping strokes, the

new president painted in his inaugural address a dark picture of present

conditions, to which disrespect of the 18th amendment and the

Volstead Act has contributed, declaring that 'most malign' of the

---

[246] Ibid.

[247] Ibid.

[248] "Prohibition: America's Failed 'Noble Experiment,'" CBS News, June 12, 2012, accessed March 6, 2017, http://www.cbsnews.com/news/prohibition-americas-failed-noble-experiment/.

dangers facing the country today is 'disregard and disobedience of

law.'"[249]

After prohibition was enacted, the presidents who served didn't

appear to follow the requirements of the law. Congress passed a special

bill to allow President Woodrow Wilson to physically transfer his

extensive collection of wine given that people who owned alcohol prior

to prohibition were allowed to keep it. Still, it was confusing as to why

President Wilson had vintages from 1922 to 1928 in his collection, since

selling alcohol was considered illegal during those years.[250]

President Harding vetoed the original Volstead Act, but was

overridden by Congress. President Harding may have had the last laugh

in that he was known for entertaining guests at the White House with

---

[249] T. Stokes, "Hoover Inaugurated, Calls for New Spirit Obeying Law," UPI Archives, United Press International, March 4, 1929, accessed March 8, 2017, http://www.upi.com/Archives/1929/03/04/Hoover-inaugurated-calls-for-new-spirit-of-obeying-law/5804975413100/.
[250] L. Bramen, "October 28, 1919: The Day That Launched a Million Speakeasies," *Smithsonian Magazine*, October 28, 2010, accessed March 8, 2017, http://www.smithsonianmag.com/arts-culture/october-28-1919-the-day-that-launched-a-million-speakeasies-103412698/.

plenty of liquor available to invited guests.[251]

President Hoover empowered the Wickersham Commission to study prohibition, and he endorsed the commission's findings. "On January 20, 1931, Hoover released the report announcing with approval that 'the commission, by a large majority does not favor the repeal of the Eighteenth Amendment...I am in accord with this view."[252] A closer look at the Wickersham Commission report conclusions, however, reveal a different side of the argument. "Others of the commission are convinced that it has been demonstrated that Prohibition under the 18th Amendment is unenforceable."[253] It was a law that the government wasn't sure how to enforce and one the people didn't want.

Ironically, it appeared the number of places that sold alcohol (illegally at the time) increased to levels higher than before prohibition was enacted.[254] This is a classic case of psychological reactance. When

[251] "Warren Harding," Bio, www.bio.com, accessed March 8, 2017, http://www.biography.com/people/warren-g-harding-9328336#synopsis.
[252] Stokes, "Hoover Inaugurated, Calls for New Spirit Obeying Law."
[253] Wickersham, G. (1931). Report on the Enforcement of the Prohibition Laws of the United States, National Commission on Law Observance and Enforcement, January 7, 1931. Accessed October 8, 2017 https://www.ncjrs.gov/pdffiles1/Digitization/44540NCJRS.pdf
[254] H. Levine, "The Birth of American Alcohol Control: Prohibition, the

people had one of their basic freedoms taken away, they responded

with great emotion. The same type of thing can happen in the

workplace. If you are aware of the things, duties, and tasks that have

great importance to your followers, you may be able to avoid or better

manage their psychological reactance.

Power Elite and the Problem of Lawlessness," *Contemporary Drug Problems* 12 (Spring, 1985): 63–115, accessed March 8, 2017, http://qcpages.qc.cuny.edu/~hlevine/The-Birth-of-American-Alcohol-Control.pdf

40. The Humble Leader: President Garfield's Lessons on Humility

What are your favorite character traits of leadership? Do you think

a leader should be inspiring? Maybe your favorite type of leader is

confident and assertive? What about the people who failed as leaders?

What were the character traits that caused them to fail so miserably? If

you had to list your most important leadership character traits, what

would you write down?

Humility is probably not the first character trait that comes to mind

when you are asked to think of leadership, but recent studies show that

being humble is of great importance. "One study of Fortune 1000

executives found that one important factor which lifted leaders from

'good to great' was modesty."[255] Leaders who are humble are more self-

aware. "Researchers observed that the intellectually humble have a

constant desire to learn and improve. They embrace ambiguity and the

unknown. They like getting new information. They even enjoy finding

out when they are wrong. And when in trouble, they're more willing to

---

[255] J. Stillman, "The Unexpected Trait That Moves Leaders from Good to Great," Inc., August 12, 2014, accessed February 28, 2017, http://www.inc.com/jessica-stillman/the-unexpected-trait-that-moves-leaders-from-good-to-great.html.

accept help."[256]

The benefits of humble leadership also extend to followers.

"Humble CEOs were found to have reduced pay disparity between

themselves and their staff. They dispersed their power. They hired more

diverse management teams, and they give staff the ability to lead and

innovate. Humble leaders have less employee turnover, higher

employee satisfaction, and they improve the company's overall

performance."[257] A humble leader is able to create stronger social and

emotional connections to his or her followers, which results in increased

engagement.

James Garfield was the man who did not want to be president.

President Garfield went to the Republican convention in 1880 as

senator-elect from the State of Ohio with the intention of supporting his

good friend, John Sherman. He gave a speech in support of Sherman on

the convention floor, but the speech was so moving, members

---

[256] A. Merryman, "Leaders Are More Powerful When They're Humble.
New Research Shows," *Washington Post*, December 8, 2016, accessed
February 28, 2017, https://www.washingtonpost.com/news/inspired-
life/wp/2016/12/08/leaders-are-more-powerful-when-theyre-humble-
new-research-shows/?utm_term=.97e2eb3e52d9.
[257] Ibid.

coalesced around a Garfield nomination.[258] Despite pleas for the

convention members to forego drafting him as their nominee, President

Garfield was selected as the republican nominee on the thirty-sixth

ballot.[259]

President Garfield served nine terms in the House of

Representatives prior to becoming president. On the eve of his

inauguration, Garfield said to his friends, "This honor comes to me

unsought, I have never had the presidential fever, not for a day."[260]

Through his efforts and hard work, President Garfield earned a

reputation for conciliation in Congress because of the way he could get

competing parties to see different perspectives. President Garfield

never sought nor took credit for his ability to get competing parties to

collaborate innately, understanding how humility led to progress, which

was why he went out of his way to fill his cabinet with representatives

from competing factions in the Republican Party.

---

[258] B. Marshall, "The Singular Humility of America's Only Ordained President," CT Pastors, April 2016, accessed February 28, 2017, http://www.christianitytoday.com/pastors/2016/april-web-exclusives/singular-humility-of-americas-only-ordained-president.html.
[259] J. Jacoby, "The Man Who Didn't Want To Be President," Boston Globe, February 16, 2014, accessed February 28, 2017, https://www.bostonglobe.com/opinion/2014/02/16/the-man-who-didn-want-president/T2emamfm4EMUEiEoLrVZvO/story.html.
[260] Ibid.

President Garfield planned on carrying his humble leadership style to the presidential office. "I shall greatly rely upon the wisdom and patriotism of Congress and of those who may share with me the responsibilities and duties of the administration and, above all, upon our efforts to promote the welfare of this great people and their government."[261] Unfortunately, President Garfield was never able to accomplish his vision as he succumbed to an assassin's gunshot wounds barely six months after taking office.

One of the best ways to show humility is to admit your mistakes. While it may be natural for us to want to avoid such an admission for fear of losing follower's confidence, doing so just might improve your leadership credibility. "When you're willing to share your own missteps, and how you dealt with them and recovered from them, you earn trust from your team."[262]

Humility is easily understood but not so easily accomplished. Admitting failure, listening to other's opinions, acknowledging when

---

[261] J. Garfield, Inauguration Speech, March 4, 1881, accessed February 28, 2017, http://www.bartleby.com/124/pres36.html.
[262] G. Moran, "6 Ways Humility Can Make You a Better Leader," Fast Company, August 11, 2014, accessed February 28, 2017, https://www.fastcompany.com/3034144/hit-the-ground-running/6-ways-humility-can-make-you-a-better-leader.

others were correct, and being open to change are challenging for any leader. Humble leaders, however, have found a way to embrace these challenges. These leaders acknowledge and accept the fact they don't know and can't do everything. Like President Garfield, they understand that there are people out there who have important ideas that can help make things better. As a leader, you control whether your ego is willing to allow you to listen or not.

41. Analysis Paralysis: The Bane of President Taft

Do you struggle when it comes time for you to make decisions? Do you find yourself repeatedly reviewing the pros and cons of each and every choice? Why do you think you hesitate? Are you afraid you might make a bad decision? What are the consequences if you make such a decision? Are these consequences much different than making no decision at all?

With so much information available to you, making a decision should be simpler as you now can look at the decision from so many different angles. Yet despite being in the information age, you are probably still making incorrect decisions as the leader. How is that possible?

What the digital age has given us, apart from previous generations, is too much information. Surprisingly, all of this available data can cause something called choice paralysis, which is described as your inability to choose an option due to the belief that there will eventually be even more information available to allow a clear choice.

In a classic study done by Columbia business professor Sheena Iyengar, people who walked through a grocery store were offered either six or twenty-four different flavors of jam to taste. On average,

customers tried two flavors and were given a coupon for purchase.

What the study found is that people who were presented with only six

jars of jam to taste were significantly more likely to purchase a jar than

those who were presented with twenty-four different flavors to try.

Professor Iyengar concluded that having so many choices led consumers

to a state of indecision, whereas fewer choices led to action.[263]

President William Taft was always considered a kind gentleman,

and when President Teddy Roosevelt left office, he heartily

recommended Taft to be the next US president. President Taft promised

to follow President Roosevelt's examples and programs, but in every

Presidency, a time comes where the person sitting in the office is forced

to make his or her own decisions.

Advisors to President Taft started to notice that it would take him

an abnormally long time to make a decision. These delays caused some

governmental operations to grind to a halt while they waited for

President Taft to act. Eventually, department heads were forced to

---

[263] A. Tugend, "Too Many Choices: A Problem That Can Paralyze," *The New York Times*, February 26, 2010, accessed March 6, 2017, https://mobile.nytimes.com/2010/02/27/your-money/27shortcuts.html.

repeatedly ask President Taft if he had made a decision on what they

had brought before him. When asked how he got through his work,

President Taft deftly replied that he didn't.[264]

President Taft was often praised for his judicious mind as he always

sought a clear analysis of the advantages and disadvantages of the

choices that lay before him. A person in an executive position, however,

does not always have the luxury of time to gauge every decision so

carefully.[265] The desire to measure out every possible outcome for each

decision caused President Taft to delay action, which caused stress to

the department heads as well as less than efficient operations.

There are psychological and social stigmas attached to people who

make bad or incorrect decisions, and these stigmas have resulted in

learned behavior. "Our brains have learned to associate pain with

making an incorrect decision."[266] This association can cause you to delay

action in the hopes that something more concrete can lead you to an

---

[264] "President Taft," *The Atlantic*, February 1912, accessed March 5, 2017, https://www.theatlantic.com/magazine/archive/1912/02/president-taft/306227/.
[265] Ibid.
[266] K. Keller. "A Bad Decision Is Better Than No Decision at All," *Entrepreneur Magazine*, April 14, 2014, accessed March 6, 2017, https://www.entrepreneur.com/article/233003.

obviously correct decision. "The control side of us is convinced that if

we have all of the puzzle pieces (of data and facts) we can put together

a perfect plan and avoid pain.[267] As you wait for the evidence to give

you the certainty you seek, you and your followers suffer high stress

because of your indecision. President Theodore Roosevelt, the

predecessor of President Taft and the one who endorsed Taft, may have

said it best when he was attributed with this quote. "In any moment of

decision, the best thing you can do is the right thing, the next best thing

is the wrong thing, and the worst thing you can do is nothing."[268] As you

lead, are you prepared to act even when you don't have all the

information you want?

---

[267] Ibid.

[268] T. Roosevelt, "Theodore Roosevelt Quotes," BrainyQuote, accessed
March 6, 2017,
https://www.brainyquote.com/quotes/quotes/t/theodorero403358.ht
ml.

42. Are You Framing Your Leadership Correctly?

Have you ever had to address a problem only to find out that you

misdiagnosed the root cause of the issue? Were your followers relying

on you to provide a fix? Did you or your followers become frustrated

when your initial idea didn't work? What would have happened if you

had taken the time to change your perspective?

In 1981, Daniel Kahneman and Amos Tversky asked six hundred

people to imagine a deadly disease had infected their bodies. Further,

the participants were told there was a medical treatment for the

disease but it was risky. Seventy-two percent of people polled were

willing to risk the consequences of the medical treatment when they

were given these odds, "A 33% chance of saving all 600 people, 66%

possibility of saving no one." When the same treatment was framed, "A

33% chance no people will die, 66% probability that all 600 will die,"

only 22 percent of participants opted for the medical treatment.[269] By

simply changing how the treatment was worded, or framed,

Kahnemann and Tversky were able to completely change the results of

---

[269] "How Thinking Works: 10 Brilliant Cognitive Psychology Studies Everyone Should Know," PsyBlog, January 2014, accessed March 9, 2017, http://www.spring.org.uk/2014/01/how-thinking-works-10-brilliant-cognitive-psychology-studies-everyone-should-know.php.

the survey. Imagine if you told your followers that your plan had a 70

percent chance to fail versus telling them that your plan has a 30

percent chance to succeed. Which frame would increase the buy-in?

The first step in the decision-making process is to frame the

problem, and it is where many leaders make mistakes. "The way a

problem is framed can profoundly influence the choices you make."[270]

Your life experiences as well as your culture, both personal and

organizational, consciously and unconsciously affect the way you frame

problems. "Because much organizational behavior occurs in complex,

chaotic, and uncertain environments, there is considerable

maneuverability with respect to shaping 'the facts.' Cues to the

environment are often ambiguous and one establishes meaning as he or

she experiences the surrounding world, creating the reality to which

they respond."[271]

---

[270] J. Hammond, R. Keeney, and H. Raiffa, "The Hidden Traps In Decision-Making," *Harvard Business Review*, September–October 1998, accessed March 15, 2017, https://hbr.org/1998/09/the-hidden-traps-in-decision-making-2.
[271] C. W. Von Bergen and J. Parnell, "Framing in Organizations: Overview, Assessment, and Implications," *Leadership & Organizational Management Journal* 2008 (2008): 83–95, accessed March 25, 2017, http://homepages.se.edu/cvonbergen/files/2012/11/Framing-in-Organizations_Overview-Assessment-and-Implications.pdf.

Framing can also be used to influence outcomes. If you frame a question in a certain way, you can influence your follower's response. "Within an organizational context, framing is a key tool leaders use— knowingly or unknowingly—to persuade and influence others, though they may be unaware of doing so."[272]

Ronald Reagan was running against President Jimmy Carter in the 1980 presidential election. In a debate between the two men, both were offered a chance to persuade voters with a final closing statement. When Reagan got his turn, he closed his session by asking the American people, "Are you better off than you were four years ago?" President Reagan tapped into a concept known as psychological accounting—an outcome is framed in terms of the direct consequences of an act or whether an outcome is evaluated with respect to a previous balance.[273] By framing the election with that question, Reagan easily outdistanced Carter to win the presidency.

On June 11, 1963, Alabama governor George Wallace attempted to block integration efforts at the University of Alabama by

---

[272] Ibid.
[273] S. Plous, *The Psychology of Judgment and Decision Making* (New York: McGraw-Hill Higher Education, 2007).

making a futile stand at the door. In his address to the nation, President Kennedy framed the problem in such a way that the civil-rights issue attacked core American freedoms. "We preach freedom around the world but are we to say to the world and...to each other that this is the land of the free except for the Negroes...?"[274] Shortly after President Kennedy framed the problem in this way, civil rights legislation was introduced and ultimately passed after his death.

How you frame problems can dictate the level and accuracy of your followers' responses. When you seek the input of others to frame important issues, you lessen the chance of misdiagnosis by allowing perspectives other than your own to be expressed. You must be careful, however, as you can easily frame the problem in such a way that it dictates the response you seek. When a problem arises, are you going to frame the question to get your desired response or are you going to be a leader and frame the issue so that you can get the unfiltered truth from your team?

---

[274] J. Rieder, "The Day Kennedy Embraced Civil Rights—And the Story Behind It," *The Atlantic*, June 11, 2013, accessed March 9, 2017, https://www.theatlantic.com/national/archive/2013/06/the-day-president-kennedy-embraced-civil-rights-and-the-story-behind-it/276749/.

43. Do You See Your Leadership through Rose-Colored

Glasses?

How many people do you know who believe themselves to be

great leaders when every indication from their followers is that they are

not nearly as good as they think themselves to be? Why is there an

incongruence between perception and reality? Shouldn't leaders be

able to see their shortfalls? What about you? If you are/will be a leader,

what are the chances that there will be a gap in your perception of your

abilities as a leader?

Human beings have an innate need to view their actions and

decisions in the most favorable ways. "Self interest is a big driver of

behavior."[275] Can your self-interest conflict with one of your follower's

needs, and if so, what normally happens in your brain when this occurs?

"What most people don't realize is that self interest often operates at a

subconscious level. So much so that we don't even know we're

behaving in the ways that we are. We don't even realize we are being as

---

[275] S. Green, "Why Smart People Make Bad Decisions," *Harvard Business Review*, February, 2009, accessed October 27, 2016, https://hbr.org/2009/02/why-smart-people-make-bad-deci.html.

self interested as we are."[276]

To prove this point, neuroscientist Tali Sharot conducted a study to measure our optimism by gauging our reaction to the possibility of realistic yet traumatic events, such as being robbed or developing Parkinson's disease, occurring in our life. Her findings illuminated the power of self-preserving tendencies. "When the volunteers were given information that was better than they hoped or expected—say, for example, that the risk of complications in surgery was only 10 percent when they thought it was 30 percent, they adjusted closer to the new risks percentages presented. But if it was worse, they tended to ignore this information."[277] The same type of thinking occurs in leadership. When negative events occur, you naturally tend to judge yourself on your intentions, and you judge your followers on their actions. By doing so, you are subconsciously giving yourself the benefit of the doubt but not offering the same opportunity to your followers.

In the early 1830s, many different Indian tribes resided in the Southeastern United States. President Washington had initially taken an approach toward Native Americans wherein he stressed the need to

---

[276] Ibid.
[277] Hertz, "Why We Make Bad Decisions."

civilize the different tribes and assimilate them into the new American

culture. As America experienced growth, the land on which the Indians

resided became more and more valuable, which led to conflict between

settlers and Native Americans. Various states passed laws limiting

Native Americans' rights, and legal actions were brought before the

United States Supreme Court, which reaffirmed the Native Americans'

rights.[278]

Despite the Supreme Court decision, President Andrew Jackson

stated that he had no intention of doing anything to enforce the

Supreme Court decision. Prior to these legal decisions, President

Jackson, who had previously fought against Native Americans,

effectively removing them from territory they owned, signed the Indian

Removal Act in 1830, which allowed the US government to exchange

Native American–held land East of the Mississippi River for land West of

the Mississippi River. The law stated that all negotiations were to be fair

and that no Native Americans were to be forcefully removed from their

land. Once again, President Jackson ignored the law.[279]

---

[278] "Trail of Tears," History Channel, accessed February 18, 2017,
http://www.history.com/topics/native-american-history/trail-of-tears.
[279] Ibid.

In a speech to Congress, President Jackson gave his interpretation

of the "progress" of Native American removal. "It gives me pleasure to

announce to Congress that the benevolent policy of the Government,

steadily pursued for nearly thirty years, in relation to the removal of

Indians beyond the white settlements is approaching to a happy

consummation."[280] As Native Americans were forced from their lands

often by the threat of bayonet, they were marched toward Oklahoma,

escorted by the US military. Thousands of Native Americans died on the

march, but President Jackson considered the government's actions a

success. "Can it be cruel in this Government when, by events which it

cannot control, the Indian is made discontented in his ancient home to

purchase his lands, to give him a new and extensive territory, to pay the

expense of his removal, and support him for a year in his new abode?

How many thousands of our own people would gladly embrace the

opportunity of removing to the West on such conditions!"[281]

President Jackson, by his statements, felt government action was

---

[280] President Jackson's Message to Congress "On Indian Removal,"
December 6, 1830; Records of the United States Senate, 1789–1990;
Record Group 46; Records of the United States Senate, 1789–1990;
National Archives and Records Administration (NARA).
[281] Ibid.

not only necessary but also righteous. "The policy of the Generous

Government toward the red man is not only liberal, but generous."[282]

Clearly, President Jackson judged himself by his intentions and not by

the actions taken against the Native Americans. Sometimes the hardest

thing for leaders to do is to see beyond their intentions and interpret

their actions for what they are.

---

[282] Ibid.

44. Rivalry and Leadership: The Deleterious Effects

Have you ever had a rival who just stirred your emotions uncontrollably? If you were competing with this rival, how important would it be for you to win? Would you be willing to go as far as to compromise your ethical beliefs to ensure victory over your rival? Would you cheat? Would you lie? Would you bend the rules in your favor to ensure that you won? If you are the leader, what ethical message are you sending to your followers?

Studies have shown that leaders can influence behavior in both positive and negative ways. While many leaders are able to adhere to their ethical values while serving followers, others end up committing to behaviors they never would have imagined. What is it that causes leaders to choose the path of grossly unethical behavior?

It appears that when we are able to convince ourselves that we are not solely responsible for the unethical action or behavior, it is easier to pursue the action or behavior. Psychologist Philip Zimbardo noted this concept when he asked students whether they would be the one willing to pull the trigger on a firing squad or be one of five people pulling the trigger on the same firing squad with no one knowing who actually had a live bullet in their chamber as opposed to a dummy

round. "If you can diffuse responsibility, so people don't feel individually

accountable, now they will do things that they ordinarily would say, 'I

would never do that."[283] By being able to psychologically deflect

responsibility to others, we can preserve our natural need to look at

ourselves in the most favorable way possible.

Competition can cause similar effects allowing for even more

unethical behavior. In Ernst & Young's 2016 Global Fraud Survey, 10

percent of almost twenty-eight hundred executives including Chief

Financial Officers (CFO), lawyers, and compliance officers were willing to

pay cash bribes in order to obtain or retain business. In addition, 42

percent of respondents could justify unethical behavior to ensure they

met financial targets.[284] "When a person focuses attention on a goal,

their moral awareness is decreased—that is they may be 'morally

disengaged' or less focused on making moral choices while pursuing a

[283] E. Wargo, "Bad Apples or Bad Barrels? Zimbardo on 'The Lucifer Effect,'" *Observer*, August 2006, accessed November 2, 2016, http://www.psychologicalscience.org/publications/observer/2006/augu st-06/bad-apples-or-bad-barrels-zimbardo-on-the-lucifer-effect.html.
[284] "Ernst & Young 2016 Global Fraud Report," Ernst & Young, 2016, accessed November 2, 2016, http://www.ey.com/gl/en/services/assurance/fraud-investigation--- dispute-services/ey-global-fraud-survey-2016.

goal."[285]

The psychology of in-groups and out-groups also plays a role in ethical and unethical behavior by leaders. If a person, company, entity, or group is seen as a rival, they are automatically placed in an out-group status, which can lead to "justified" unethical behavior. "Moral decisions can be influenced by incidental emotions that are unrelated to the decision context."[286] With emotions added to the mixture, rivalry leads to much more volatile behavior than simple competition. "Furthermore, we find evidence that rivalry is associated with increased psychological stakes, consistent with the conceptualization used here and elsewhere, and that this helps explain why rivalry fosters increased unethical behavior."[287]

While we can certainly find examples of business leaders who exploited competition and rivalries, there may be no better example

[285] "Do Aggressive Goals Drive Unethical Behavior," W. P. Carey School of Business, Arizona State University, June 28, 2016, accessed November 4, 2016, http://research.wpcarey.asu.edu/management-entrepreneurship/do-aggressive-goals-drive-unethical-behavior/.
[286] G. Kilduff, A. Galinsky, E. Gallo, and J. Reade, "Whatever It Takes: Rivalry and Unethical Behavior," *Academy of Management Journal*, 2015, accessed November 2, 2016, https://www0.gsb.columbia.edu/mygsb/faculty/research/pubfiles/16170/Galinsky%20Rivalry%20and%20unethical%20behavior.pdf.
[287] Ibid.

than US political parties. From the outset, competition and rivalry led to

seemingly unethical behaviors. In 1800, President Thomas Jefferson

paid the editor of the *Richmond Examiner* to print anti-Federalist and

other denigrating articles about sitting President John Adams while also

praising Jefferson's presidential ability and qualifications. This behavior

caused Jefferson's followers to claim Adams was a "hideous

hermaphrodital character." President Andrew Jackson was called an

adulterer. Jackson's followers retaliated against sitting President John

Quincy Adams by calling him an "unscrupulous aristocrat" who misused

Federal monies.[288] President Kennedy asserted that Russia had more

nuclear missiles than the United States and made the assertion an

integral part of his election platform despite the assertion being

untruthful. President Nixon claimed he had no involvement in the

Watergate break-in.[289] Given these instances and the current state of

political polarization across the United States, should we be surprised by

what we have seen in the last few years?

---

[288] A. Fernandez, "Lies, Insults, And Exaggerations,: A U.S. Presidential Campaign Tradition," *Los Angeles Times*, August 21, 2016, accessed November 2, 2016, http://www.latimes.com/nation/la-na-crazy-elections-history-20160802-snap-htmlstory.html.
[289] D. Bush, "The History of Lies on the Campaign Trail," PBS, December 4, 2015, accessed November 2, 2016, http://www.pbs.org/newshour/updates/the-history-of-lies-on-the-campaign-trail/.

On October 30, 2016, US presidential candidate Hillary Clinton

claimed that FBI Director James Comey sent his letter about new

developments into her e-mails only to Republican members of the

House of Representatives.[290] Her comment is blatantly untrue as was

her initial statements about not having any classified e-mails on her

personal Internet server. On October 25, 2016, US presidential

candidate Donald Trump claimed WikiLeaks e-mails showed how the

Clinton campaign manager, John Podesta, rigged polls by oversampling

democrats in an effort to suppress voters.[291] As of yet, there are no e-

mails released by WikiLeaks to support this allegation, and Trump has

made other unsupported claims as well.

One of the most egregious examples of rivalry leading to unethical

behavior by politicians involved then-Senate Majority Leader Harry Reid

and 2012 US presidential candidate Mitt Romney. On the Senate floor,

Reid accused Romney of not paying any taxes over the previous decade.

Romney released his tax returns for 2010 and 2011, clearly showing that

---

[290] "All False Statements Involving Hillary Clinton," Politifact, November 2, 2016, accessed November 2, 2016, http://www.politifact.com/personalities/hillary-clinton/statements/byruling/false/.

[291] "All Statements Involving Donald Trump," Politifact, November 2, 2016, accessed November 2, 2016, http://www.politifact.com/personalities/donald-trump/statements/.

he had paid almost $5 million dollars in US taxes. To this day, Senator Reid refers to his false statement on the Senate floor as "one of the best things he has ever done" and refuses to retract the false allegation. Reid justifies his lie by saying, "Romney didn't win, did he?" [292]

When leaders define their in-groups in narrower terms, that is, Democrat versus Republican, instead of as a unified group, such as Americans, dedicated to improving our country, ethics are obliterated. People's sole purpose becomes to win for my group instead of looking for a more inclusive solution. It is only natural for followers to mimic their leader's unethical behavior. The mythological story of President George Washington admitting to his father that he cut down the cherry tree becomes less salient with each perpetuated lie told by our governmental leaders. Unethical behavior will dominate our behavioral decisions as long as we see leadership as a contest between rivals. Will you be the exception?

---

[292] C. Cillizza, "Harry Reid Lied About Mitt Romney's Taxes. He's Still Not Sorry," *The Washington Post*, September 15, 2016, accessed November 2, 2016, https://www.washingtonpost.com/news/the-fix/wp/2016/09/15/harry-reid-lied-about-mitt-romneys-taxes-hes-still-not-sorry/.

45. President Hayes and His Need for Psychological Cleansing

How many of you have gone through training where you were

presented with scenarios or presentations designed to teach you ethical

behavior? Were the desired answers obvious? Did you feel like the

training was a waste of time? Finally, do you consider yourself more

ethical than your peers?

Normally when groups of people are asked the last question,

almost everyone answers in the affirmative. Is there a chance, however,

that when you actually face real ethical dilemmas, you might not act in

the way that you believe you would? As much as you try, you won't

always make the correct ethical and moral decision every chance you

get. When you stray from your ethical and moral bases, your mind starts

to work in subtle ways, slowly changing the way facts are framed, so

that you can restore your ethical and moral self-image. One way you

restore your favorable self-image is through a process called

psychological cleansing, which is your selective ability to turn your usual

ethical standards on or off at will. Psychological cleansing is an aspect of

moral disengagement and is a process that allows you to behave

contrary to your moral and ethical code while still viewing yourself as an ethical and moral person.[293]

The presidential election of 1876 was a deadlocked race between

Republican Rutherford B. Hayes and Democrat Samuel L. Tilden, who

had divergent views of the United States' long-term future. Hayes

sought to further reconstruction efforts in the South while Tilden

promised to prevent former slaves from voting in the South. On the

night of the election, Hayes went to sleep thinking he had lost the

election, but when Hayes woke up the next day, he learned that

Louisiana, Florida, and South Carolina were still in play, which gave him

a chance at winning the election. Without any of those three states,

Tilden was one electoral vote shy of winning the presidency. In order to

become president, Hayes needed a clean sweep to become president.[294]

Allegations of voter fraud were coming from both sides as each

party was trying to get its respective candidate the necessary electoral

votes to win. Republicans were accused of stuffing the ballot box with

---

[293] M. Bazerman and A. Tenbrunsel, *Blind Spots: Why We Fail to Do What's Right and What to Do About It* (Princeton, NJ and Oxford: Princeton University Press, 2011), 72–73.
[294] G. King, "The Ugliest, Most Contentious Presidential Election Ever," *Smithsonian Magazine*, September 7, 2012, accessed March 8, 2017, http://www.smithsonianmag.com/history/the-ugliest-most-contentious-presidential-election-ever-28429530/.

fake votes, and Democrats were accused of harassing and intimidating former slaves so as not to allow them to vote. Rumors that voting officials in each of the three states sought or were offered bribes by the various parties began running rampant. Months passed and it seemed that both Tilden and Hayes were in position to win the presidency at various times, but ultimately a compromise was reached. If Hayes agreed to remove federal troops from the Southern states, the Democrats would not stand in the way of his presidency.[295] Rutherford B. Hayes took the presidential oath of office on March 3, 1877, and took the same oath a second time on March 5, 1877, before giving his inaugural address.[296]

In his inaugural speech, President Hayes spoke of the problems in the South. "With respect to the two different races whose peculiar relations to each other have brought upon us the deplorable complications and perplexities which exist in those States, it must be a government which guards the interests of both races carefully and equally."[297] Despite the pleas of concerned citizens, President Hayes

---

[295] Ibid.

[296] Rutherford B. Hayes Inaugural Address, www.bartleby.com, accessed March 8, 2017, http://www.bartleby.com/124/pres35.html.

[297] Ibid.

removed federal troops from Southern states. Southern state

legislatures, acting without federal supervision, started enacting laws

referred to as Jim Crow laws. These new legal regulations denied many,

if not all, civil rights to African Americans despite their legal status as US

citizens.[298]

In recounting his decision to remove federal troops and to rely on

Southern states to self-govern, President Hayes, via a letter penned in

1881, expressed satisfaction with the troop removal. "He [Hayes] wrote

that he found a country 'divided and distracted and every instance

depressed' but he left a nation united, harmonious and prosperous."[299]

President Hayes, from all accounts, seemed to be a moral and

ethical man who started his quest for the presidency looking to heal the

continuing divisions in the country while providing civil liberties and

freedoms to all former slaves. Events that transpired during the election

and his ultimate ascendancy to the presidency led President Hayes to

undergo psychological cleansing. "Our memory is selective; specifically,

---

[298] "Compromise of 1877," History Channel, accessed March 8, 2017, http://www.history.com/topics/us-presidents/compromise-of-1877.
[299] C. Booker, "Rutherford B. Hayes and the Compromise of 1877," African-Americans and the Presidency, March 8, 2017, accessed March 8, 2017, http://www.blacksandpresidency.com/rutherfordhayes.php.

we remember behaviors that support our self-image and conveniently

forget those that do not."[300] Unfortunately for you and other leaders,

followers don't rationalize your behavior and they are not nearly as

forgetful when it comes to your efforts to perform a thorough

psychological cleansing.

---

[300] Bazerman and Tenbrunsel, *Blind Spots*, 73.

46. The Salary Grab: President Grant Discovers the Need for Transparency

Have you ever had a leader who you felt was hiding something

important from you? What effect did that have on your level of

engagement at work? Did you find yourself openly or silently wondering

whether what you were being told was true or complete? Was your

workday more stressful? If you have felt this way when working for a

leader who lacked transparency, ask yourself if you are being as

transparent as you need to be, because if you aren't, isn't it likely that

your followers share similar concerns?

According to a 2014 study done by the American Psychological

Association, a full quarter of employees do not trust their employer, and

only half of the respondents believe their organization operates with

transparency.[301] "Trust and transparency have become popular

workforce demands as employees seek to be aware of what is real and

true."[302] Without an investment in transparency, a leader will not be

---

[301] A. Lavoie, "4 Reasons You Need to Embrace Transparency in the Workplace," Entrepreneur, April 28, 2015, accessed February 14, 2017, https://www.entrepreneur.com/article/245461.

[302] G. Llopis, "5 Powerful Things Happen When a Leader Is Transparent," Forbes, September 10, 2012, accessed February 12, 2017,

able to forge the bonds of trust with his or her followers.

Modern organizations are starting to recognize the need for transparency by establishing new metrics to measure executive leadership. Organizations are not only looking for success in the traditional forms of profit and performance but also increasingly seeing the importance of measuring social and ethical responsibility of which transparency is a key component.[303]

The constitutional creators allowed Congress to set their own as well as other governmental salaries believing that American citizens would be afforded the chance to hold these elected representatives accountable through the voting process. Looking throughout history, the public has both accepted federal pay raises as well as aggressively renouncing them by electing the same or different people depending on their perception of acceptance. Congress was quick to take notice when the public responded negatively to unfairly perceived pay raises and started to create ways to hide their true intentions from the public. "To

http://www.forbes.com/sites/glennllopis/2012/09/10/5-powerful-things-happen-when-a-leader-is-transparent/.

[303] J. O'Toole and W. Bennis, "A Culture of Candor," *Harvard Business Review*, June 2009, accessed February 15, 2017, https://hbr.org/2009/06/a-culture-of-candor.

protect themselves from this sort of constituent reaction, members of

Congress throughout the nineteenth century used a host of techniques

to reduce transparency and hide blame, such as improving and

enhancing non-salary perquisites, such as mileage reimbursement rates,

franking, congressional staff and retirement benefits, or passing a

smaller salary increase but 'backdating' it."[304]

Inasmuch as transparency is a key component of trust, imagine

how the general voting public felt when Congress, in the last hours of

the last day of the 1873 congressional session, attached legislation to an

appropriations bill, increasing theirs, the president's, and other

governmental officials' salaries. In addition to raising salaries,

congressional members backdated the provision by two years,

effectively giving themselves a bonus equal to their annual salary. This

was done during a time when the country was going through the throes

of a financial depression and when many congressional members were

aware they would not be returning as congressional members in

---

[304] Lee J. Alston and Jeffery A. Jenkins, Tomas Nonnenmacher, "Who Should Govern Congress? Access to Power and the Salary Grab of 1873," *The Journal of Economic History* 66, no. 3 (2006): 674–706.

1874.[305]

After President Grant signed the bill, the media discovered the "salary grab" and reported it to the American public. Immediately, there was substantial public outrage against congressional members as well as President Grant.[306] The people felt like they were being tricked, which lessened trust and disconnected the bond between leader and follower. The 1874 Congress, where 50 percent of its members were newly elected, quickly repealed the pay raise, only allowing the pay raises for the president and the Supreme Court justices to remain.[307]

When Congress and President Grant tried to slip this pay raise quietly past the American public, they weren't acting transparently, which led to a violation of trust. Leaders who choose to selectively hide information from their followers jeopardize mutual respect. Engaged employees are more emotionally committed to an organization and will work harder on its behalf if they respect senior leadership.[308] Are you

---

[305] Ibid.
[306] Ibid.
[307] Ibid.
[308] V. Lipman, "Why Transparency Is Always the Best Leadership Policy," *Psychology Today*, July 25, 2013, accessed February 14, 2017, https://www.psychologytoday.com/blog/mind-the-

being as transparent as you should be with your followers?

---

manager/201307/why-transparency-is-always-the-best-leadership-policy.

47. The Buck Stops Here...Or Does It?

When something goes wrong, who gets the blame? When something goes right, who gets the credit? Are you a leader who quickly looks at others to find fault when things go wrong, or are you a leader who is willing to accept blame even though you may not be the one who is at fault? Likewise, do you happily accept the accolades, or do you ensure your followers get the credit? Whether the success or failure was yours or your followers, what kind of impact would your decision have?

President Harry S. Truman had a well-known sign on his desk that read, "The buck stops here." Many people interpreted this sign to mean that blame or credit belongs to the leader, but as it turns out, your brain plays an active role when deciding how to distribute blame or credit. Researchers at Duke University found interesting brain activity when doing scans where people were given scenarios involving a leader being blamed for a problem and a leader being given credit for something good. "Emotions drive ascriptions of intentionality for negative consequences while the consideration of statistical norms leads to the denial for intentionality of positive circumstances."[309] Giving credit to

someone for doing a good job does not ignite the emotional fires like

blaming someone for a disaster does.

Self-esteem plays an important role in how we function and has a

role in distributing both blame and credit. "Not surprisingly, thinking

about failure temporarily decreases self-esteem whereas thinking about

success temporarily bolsters it."[310] When thinking about other's success,

we do not get the same feelings of elation as we do when we think of

our successes. In fact, other people's successes can make us perceive

that we are somehow deficient. Even though leaders are supposed to

rejoice when members of your team succeed, can you recall an instance

where a follower did something special, and even though you may have

been appreciative in public, there was a pang of jealousy hidden inside

of you?

---

[309] L. Ngo, M. Kelly, C. Coutlee, R. M. Carter, W. Sinnott-Armstrong, and S. Huettel, "Two Distinct More Mechanisms for Ascribing and Denying Intentionality," Scientific Reports, December 4, 2015, accessed September 27, 2016, http://www.nature.com/articles/srep17390.
[310] C. Routledge, "The Secrets to a Meaningful Life, Part III: The Importance of Self-Esteem," Psychology Today, May 27, 2010, accessed September 28, 2016, https://www.psychologytoday.com/blog/more-mortal/201005/the-secrets-meaningful-life-part-iii-the-importance-self-esteem.

Likewise, when failure happens, blaming yourself is a threat to your

self-esteem. "Whether you call it projection, denial, or displacement,

blame helps you preserve your sense of self-esteem by avoiding

awareness of your own flaws or failings."[311] Blaming someone else for

the problem is a natural response, but is it what a leader should do?

President Herbert Hoover served when the United States' Great

Depression ignited. President Hoover reacted to the problem and took

an active role in trying to respond to the debilitating market crash.

Hoover met with business leaders and got them to commit to $1.8

billion in new construction projects. President Hoover also urged federal

departments to speed up construction projects while asking Congress

for a $160 million tax cut. While hindsight shows the effects of President

Hoover's actions differently, the New York Times in the spring of 1930

praised President Hoover's actions in these difficult times. "No one in

his place could have done more." Yet despite his work, President

Hoover is frequently assigned the blame for the decade-long

---

[311] S. Krauss-Whitbourne, "5 Reasons We Play the Blame Game...But Rarely Win," *Psychology Today*, September 19, 2015, accessed September 28, 2016, https://www.psychologytoday.com/blog/fulfillment-any-age/201509/5-reasons-we-play-the-blame-game.

depression."[312]

In the election of 1932, Franklin Roosevelt soundly defeated the

incumbent, Hoover. "FDR successfully pinned everything on Hoover in

re-election upon re-election."[313] Years later, President Roosevelt's aides

acknowledged that many of the "New Deal" programs were closely

modeled after programs first proposed by President Hoover.[314] Because

of the way President Roosevelt openly blamed former President Hoover

for America's problems, neither man cared for each other. It wasn't

until President Roosevelt's successor, Harry Truman, installed former

President Hoover as the person to oversee Europe's reconstruction

efforts did some of Hoover's bitterness towards President Roosevelt

---

[312] R. Smith and T. Walch, "The Ordeal of Herbert Hoover," National Archives, Summer 2004, accessed May 16, 2017, https://www.archives.gov/publications/prologue/2004/summer/hoover-1.html.
[313] P. Kengor, "The Presidential Blame Game," The Center for Vision and Values, Grove City College, February 18, 2013, accessed May 16, 2017, http://www.visionandvalues.org/2013/02/the-presidential-blame-game/.
[314] "Herbert Hoover on the Great Depression and New Deal, 1931–1933," the Gilder-Lehrman Institute of American History, 2009, accessed May 16, 2017, https://www.gilderlehrman.org/history-by-era/new-deal/resources/herbert-hoover-great-depression-and-new-deal-1931%E2%80%931933.

fade.[315]

Since President Roosevelt's time, there have been many occasions where a sitting president has blamed his predecessor for any number of problems. Over the last few decades, Presidents Clinton, Bush, Obama, and Trump have both cast blame or seen their successors attribute problems to previous presidents. In some ways, blaming others for your problems is easier than looking at yourself as the potential cause of the problem.

The path of failure is lined with good intentions. No matter what you do, no matter how hard you work, you are destined to fail at certain things. When you do, your followers will take notice. They will want to know whether you are going to "pass the buck" or allow "the buck to stop" with you.

---

[315] Kengor, "The Presidential Blame Game."

48. President Washington: When Moral Leadership Bested Presidential Power

Are there leaders in your organization who thrive on positions of

power? Do these leaders revel in their power while taking extreme joy

in wielding said power? Why does a leader allow power to engulf

his/her personality, turning him/her from a caring and concerned leader

to one who relies on fear and intimidation? As a follower, how do you

feel when your leader arbitrarily uses his or her power for personal gain

or even personal amusement?

In some ways, leadership is all about power. Traditional corporate

structures are based in top-down command and control relationships,

whereby the person in the higher position is granted a level of power

over others. Power can go both ways, however. While power can make

you confident and more assertive, desired traits for leaders, power can

also cause you to focus on your own desires at the expense of your

followers.[316]

A study done by University of Toronto management Professor

---

[316] R. Riggio, "How Power Corrupts Leaders," *Psychology Today*, August 8, 2009, accessed February 28, 2017, https://www.psychologytoday.com/blog/cutting-edge-leadership/200908/how-power-corrupts-leaders.

Katherine DeCelles revealed how moral identity shapes a person's

response to wielding power. "Peoples sense of 'moral identity'—the

degree to which they thought it was important to their sense of self to

be 'caring,' 'compassionate,' 'fair,' 'generous,' and so on—shaped their

responses to feelings of power."[317] Leaders who are emotionally

intelligent and work from a high moral identity are better prepared to

withstand the allure of self-dealing that comes from holding power over

others. "What power does is that it liberates the true self to emerge."[318]

Without constraints or additional perspectives, you will normally choose

options that clearly have your self-interest in mind.

On March 4, 1797, President Washington did something

amazing. He relinquished the presidency after two terms and returned

to his farm in Virginia to live out his remaining years. This act was so

profound, it stunned a great number of people, including England's King

George III, who said after learning of President Washington's plans to

---

[317] C. Shea, "Why Power Corrupts," *Smithsonian Magazine*, October 2012, accessed February 28, 2017, http://www.smithsonianmag.com/science-nature/why-power-corrupts-37165345/.
[318] B. Resnick, "How Power Corrupts The Mind," *The Atlantic*, July 9, 2013, accessed February 28, 2017, https://www.theatlantic.com/health/archive/2013/07/how-power-corrupts-the-mind/277638/.

step down, "If he does that, he will be the greatest man in the world."[319]

President Washington had worked all of his life to establish his character and reputation. Washington could have easily deemed himself king once the Revolutionary War ended, and most people would have accepted such a declaration. Washington almost assuredly would have been elected for a third presidential term if he had chosen to run, but President Washington despised monarchies.[320] His moral identity was based on his character. "He believed in a republic of free citizens with a government based on consent and established to protect the rights of life, liberty and property."[321]

Throughout history, there have been leaders who, once they seized power, relinquished it only upon death or military defeat. The example set by President Washington was a seminal moment for an emerging country, which was formed based on the principles of personal freedoms. In relinquishing power, President Washington set the tone for generations of American leaders to follow. President Abraham

---

[319] D. Boaz, "The Man Who Would Not Be King," Cato Institute, February 20, 2006, accessed February 28, 2017, https://www.cato.org/publications/commentary/man-who-would-not-be-king.
[320] Ibid.
[321] Ibid.

Lincoln once said, "Nearly all men can stand adversity, but if you want to test a man's character, give him power."[322] Could you serve like President Washington while also passing President Lincoln's litmus test of power?

---

[322] Shea, "Why Power Corrupts."

49. President Clinton and How Your Brain Lies

Have you ever had a leader who told you an unnecessary and

outright, bold-faced lie? What did that do to the leader's credibility? Did

the fact that the leader was unwilling to tell you the truth affect your

motivation? Once lied to, what are the chances that you would ever

willingly follow this leader again?

One of the things that has always confounded students in our

leadership classes is how some so-called leaders lie and expect you not

to know they are lying. This is especially difficult in law enforcement,

inasmuch as many of the people who are being led have advanced

training in lie-detection techniques. Knowing this, why do leaders lie?

Recently, a group of scientists studied the brain's reaction to

lying in order to see if there is a biological component in play when we

decide to lie. Early results suggest that there may be such a connection

with the amygdala in our brains, which are associated with emotion.

"When we lie for personal gain, our amygdala produces a negative

feeling that limits the extent to which we are prepared to lie. However, this response fades as we continue to lie"[323] Does that mean the more

we lie, the more comfortable we become with telling something other

than the truth?

It is no secret that the human body adapts to its environment.

Remember a time where you went out in the cold with a jacket, and

before long, you removed your jacket as your body adjusted to the

temperature. Our inner body also has similar mechanisms. For example,

if you were sitting upright and tilted to either side, eventually that

would become your equilibrium, and you would feel that you were

sitting straight up, even though your position hadn't changed. Lying

seems to have a similar effect.

In 1998, President William Jefferson Clinton denied having an

affair with an intern named Monica Lewinsky. When news reporters and

other interested parties uncovered the relationship, a scandal was born.

Various investigations into the matter found proof that President

Clinton's statements were outright lies. The US government appointed a

special counsel to look into the possibility that President Clinton lied

---

[323] J. Ravitz, "Lying May Be Your Brain's Fault, Honestly," CNN, October 24, 2016, accessed October 24, 2016, http://www.cnn.com/2016/10/24/health/brain-lying/index.html.

under oath when being interviewed on another matter. In his

testimony, President Clinton denied having sex with Lewinsky despite

evidence existing to the contrary.

Since that time, President Clinton has answered questions

about the Lewinsky affair, and if we study his responses, they have

gradually changed over time. In 2001, former President Clinton

admitted to giving misleading answers in a deposition. In his own words,

President Clinton, despite the contrary evidence, still did not admit to

lying. "I tried to walk a fine line between acting lawfully and testifying

falsely, but I now recognize that I did not fully accomplish that goal and

certain of my responses to questions about Ms. Lewinsky were false."[324]

Given that President Clinton has been asked about Monica Lewinsky

thousands of times, should we be surprised that he still can't say he lied

in his deposition?

In some ways, our brains act in selfish ways. In order to

preserve our self-image, we often lie to ourselves. Whenever we do

---

[324] H. Kennedy, "President Clinton Admits He Lied Under Oath About His Affair with Monica Lewinsky," *New York Daily News*, January 19, 2016, originally published January 20, 2001, accessed October 27, 2016, http://www.nydailynews.com/news/politics/bill-feds-cut-dealsurrenders-law-license-escape-ind-article-1.904790.

something foolish, our natural reaction is to compensate by minimizing our role or deflecting the reason for our action. As the cited study showed, the more we lie, the more our brains get used to lying. If a leader is known as someone who is a liar, what are the chances that anyone will follow that leader?

50. Lessons on Conflict: President Reagan and General Secretary Gorbachev

How do you deal with conflict? Do you avoid it? Would you rather

ignore it and pretend it doesn't exist? Would confronting the root cause

of the conflict be the best approach? When you address conflict, do you

have a clear strategy or approach to resolution? If you were to self-

assess, how much of your strategy and approach involves you winning

the conflict?

Conflict and even the fear of conflict can paralyze leaders, but the

effects of such conflict and fear have ramifications for followers as well.

"The fear of conflict and ineffective conflict strategies cause employees

to settle into a state of helplessness similar to what hostages feel."[325]

Entering into dialogue instead of conversation is a powerful tool for

conflict resolution.

A leader who enters into dialogue is more interested in

understanding the root problem of the conflict as opposed to superficial

---

[325] G. Kohlrieser, "Conflict To Dialogue, Use Hostage Negotiation
Techniques," www.georgekohlriser.com, 2017, accessed February 18,
2017,
http://www.georgekohlrieser.com/userfiles/file/articles/6.GK_ConflictT
oDialogue.pdf.

details. Taking such an approach leads to greater truths. "In dialogue, we experience ourselves as bonded to the person to whom we are speaking making understanding and meaning flow beyond words."[326] Dialogue is easier said than done, however. Leaders who feel the need to prove a point or ensure their point of view is correct fail to enter into dialogue, which either sustains conflict or at best, significantly delays resolution.

Some of the methods to block dialogue are passivity, discounting, redefining, and overdetailing. When a leader refuses to engage or is nonresponsive, the follower sees no interest in conflict resolution. The same effect occurs when the leader says disparaging things to belittle another person as they discuss issues or problems. Likewise when a leader manipulates the conversation to a more advantageous frame, mind-sets are changed and resolution is avoided. Finally when a leader provides too many details, the information overload doesn't allow followers to process what is truly relevant.[327]

In the run up to his campaign to win the presidential election of 1980, Ronald Reagan often referred to the Soviet Union as the "Evil

---

[326] Ibid.
[327] Ibid.

Empire." It was a chilling start for such competing nations when it came time to negotiate differences. In turn, General Secretary Mikhail Gorbachev and other Soviet representatives reciprocated by referring to President Reagan as a "B" movie Hollywood star. As they entered into negotiations concerning nuclear disarmament, there was plenty of mistrust and a general mood of conflict.

To both President Reagan's and General Secretary Gorbachev's surprise, the two men started to find common ground despite still harboring palpable suspicions. In Reykjavik where both President Reagan and General Secretary Gorbachev were negotiating a reduction in nuclear armaments, President Reagan made a bold offer that completely transformed the relationship between the two men. President Reagan finally entered into a dialogue when he suggested that the two men address each other by their first names. General Secretary Gorbachev recalled the meeting. "I remember the episode when we were sitting down together, President Reagan and me, and he said, 'I think the time has come for us to be on a first name basis. Call me Ron."[328] By opening a new and more intimate dialogue, both President

---

[328] W. Hoge, "Once Red, Mr. Green Is a Hero Anywhere But Home," *The New York Times*, October 23, 2004, accessed February 18, 2017,

Reagan and General Secretary Gorbachev were able to negotiate

landmark treaties, which made the world safer.

When asked by George Shultz, President Reagan's Secretary of

State, what was the turning point in the Cold War between the United

States and the Soviet Union, General Secretary Gorbachev responded

immediately by saying, "Reykjavik." Further discussion indicated that

the meeting in Reykjavik was the first time the two leaders entered into

a dialogue searching for each other's hopes, dreams, and visions. While

they certainly didn't agree on every point, they didn't fall into the traps

to deter and prevent dialogue. Because of their newfound trust and

understanding generated by dialogue, the two leaders were able to

discard the animus of previous assumptions and work toward goals that

were mutually acceptable.[329] Are you, as the leader, taking the time to

enter into true dialogue with your followers, or are you doing your best

to avoid meaningful conversations by being passive, discounting,

redefining, and overdetailing?

---

http://www.nytimes.com/2004/10/23/world/europe/once-red-mr-green-is-a-hero-anywhere-but-at-home.html?_r=0.
[329] D. Yankelovich, *The Magic of Dialogue: Transforming Conflict into Cooperation* (New York: Simon & Schuster, 1999).

51. Leadership and Mindfulness: The President Lincoln and President Roosevelt Way

Do you have trouble balancing the need to spend time with your

followers and accomplishing the tasks required of you? Have you found

yourself constantly checking your phone or e-mail when you get home?

Is the connected life making you stressed out?

With so many interconnected electronic devices, we are immersed

in our work like never before. Over half of Americans who work fifty

plus hours per week do not use their vacation time.[330] We often fall into

the trap of believing that our presence is essential. We conjure excuses

as to why we should forego vacations, such as the extra burden our

absence would place on others as well as believing that absence can

lead to missed promotional opportunities. Even if we go on vacation, we

don't sever our connectivity to the workplace. A poll conducted by NPR,

the Robert Wood Johnson Foundation, and the Harvard T. H. Chan

School of Public Health found that of the people who do take vacation,

30 percent of them still do significant amounts of work while gone from

---

[330] P. Neighmond, "Overworked Americans Are not Taking the Vacation They've Earned," NPR, July 12, 2016, accessed August 15, 2016, http://www.npr.org/sections/health-shots/2016/07/12/485606970/overworked-americans-arent-taking-the-vacation-theyve-earned.

the office.[331]

Spending so much time at work can be harmful to your health.

Working continuously can cause stress to build up, which in turn, affects

your body and mind. Taking respites from work, even short ones, has

proven to increase people's health and wellness. "Experiences of

relaxation and detachment from work positively influenced health and

wellness even after returning home."[332] Even the best of workers

benefit from taking time away from work.

Presidents Lincoln and Franklin Roosevelt served during

tremendous times of crises in American History. Lincoln was leading the

North in the Civil War and Roosevelt was battling against the Great

Depression and a World War. Both men, who were naturally

melancholy, could have folded under the stress and the pressure, but in

fact, both men thrived. How did they succeed in the midst of such

national duress?

---

[331] Ibid.
[332] J. de Bloom, S. A. Guerts, and M. A. Kompler, "Effects of Short
Vacations, Vacation Activities, and Experiences on Employee Health and
Well-Being," *Stress Health* 28, no. 4 (2012): 305–18.
doi:10.1002/smi.1434, Epub 2011 Dec 28, accessed August 15, 2016,
http://www.ncbi.nlm.nih.gov/pubmed/22213478.

While both men had a natural gift for communicating difficult concepts in ways that were easily understandable, they each understood the necessity of carving out time where they could get away from the stress of the times. President Lincoln would entertain people into the late-night hours by telling entertaining stories, which made him and his guests laugh out loud. President Roosevelt proclaimed a nightly cocktail hour where no guest could discuss current day events. If no one were present for a cocktail hour, President Roosevelt would work with his stamp collection.[333]

These short respites recharged these leaders and allowed them to function at higher levels. Granted, these leaders didn't have the connectivity that is prevalent in the world today, but even if they did, they would have found a way to carve out some time to alleviate their stress. Don't you have the same options today? Maybe you won't take the time off for vacation, but you can occasionally turn your phone off in order to give yourself a short but much needed respite from work.

---

[333] D. Coutu, "Leadership Lessons from Abraham Lincoln," *Harvard Business Review*, April 2009, accessed August 15, 2016, https://hbr.org/2009/04/leadership-lessons-from-abraham-lincoln.

52. "Taking the Time" to Lead like Lincoln

If you were to assess your relationship with your organizational leader, would you be able to say that you have a personal and emotional connection with that leader? If not, do you wish that you had such a connection? If yes, does having such a connection impact your work performance? If you do have a personal and emotional connection, how did you feel when your leader saw that you gave less than your best effort? What do you think your followers would say about you if they were asked these same questions?

President Theodore Roosevelt once said, "Nobody cares how much you know until they know how much you care." Studies have shown that a leader who cares about his or her followers can increase employee engagement. "Employee engagement is a direct reflection of how employees feel about their relationship with the boss."[334] Engagement is borne through intrinsic motivation, and if you have created an environment where there is no personal connection between you and your follower, there will be lower levels of employee

---

[334] D. Crim and G. Seijts, "What Engages the Employees the Most OR, the Ten C's of Employee Engagement," *Ivey Business Journal*, March/April 2006, accessed September 9, 2016, www.iveybusinessjournal.com/publication/what-engages-employees-the-most-or-the-ten-cs-of-employee-engagement/.

engagement causing decreased efficiency and productivity in the

organization.

Leaders who are able to successfully connect with their followers,

however, enter into the realm of transformational leadership. The four

areas of transformational leadership, as defined by Bernard Bass, are

intellectual stimulation, inspirational motivation, idealized influence,

and individualized consideration. Bass believed leaders who could

command these traits would be able to increase intrinsic motivation,

but if you were to look closely at the descriptions provided by Bass,

aren't they based on a personal connection between leader and

follower? "For transformational leaders, followers are more than just

employees; they are people."[335]

President Lincoln made it a point to regularly meet with

constituents even during the midst of the Civil War. Cabinet members

were frustrated by Lincoln's meetings with civilians wondering why the

President would make time for ordinary people when the fate of the

---

[335] E. Wiltshire, "Transformational Leadership: What's Your Motivation," Leadership Advance Online, School of Global Leadership & Entrepreneurship, Regent University, Issue XXII, 2012, accessed September 9, 2016, http://www.regent.edu/acad/global/publications/lao/issue_22/3Wiltshire_motivation_lao_22.pdf.

entire United States was at risk. President Lincoln understood that as

the leader of the United States, he represented the entire country, not

just those with wealth and positions of importance. In this way,

President Lincoln increased engagement and motivated others by

remembering that he was once one of them. "I must never forget the

popular assemblage from which I come."[336]

President Lincoln also made it a point to travel to see the

northern troops whenever he could. Sometimes the journeys were

painstakingly long, but President Lincoln never relented. On more than

twelve occasions, President Lincoln traveled to an active battlefield right

after conflict.[337] Lincoln understood how his mere presence helped

increase the connection between leader and follower as well as the

effect his presence had on the intrinsic motivation of the union soldiers.

One soldier said of President Lincoln, "Lincoln's warm smile was a

reflection of his honest, kindly heart; but deeper under the surface than

---

[336] The Moral Leadership of American Presidents," *Westmont Magazine,* Westmont, College, Summer 2015, accessed September 9, 2016, http://blogs.westmont.edu/magazine/2015/11/30/the-moral-leadership-of-american-presidents/.
[337] Ibid.

that...were the unmistakable signs of care."[338]

In one of our classes, there was an executive who understood the need to meet with his followers but complained that he couldn't afford the time to meet with others due to the amount of work required of his position. A colleague from Alaska questioned how that leader couldn't afford to make time to meet with his followers. The Alaskan leader related how he had to fly three hundred miles a couple of times per month in order to meet with his followers who were in remote offices. The Alaskan colleague believed that it was absolutely necessary for a leader to carve out the time in his or her schedule to connect with followers even if it meant that he or she had to delegate tasks that he or she would rather keep to him- or herself. Connecting, to this leader, was the most important thing he had to do.

Frequently, leaders attribute the lack of employee engagement to the follower, but if you were to look a little more closely at the issue, you might realize that you, as a leader, have a much bigger role in employee engagement than you might think. Using President Lincoln's example, have you taken the time to establish connections with your

[338] Crowley, "The Leadership Genius of Abraham Lincoln."

followers? If not, what's your excuse?

Bonus Chapters from Michael Bret Hood's *Eat More Ice Cream*: *A Succinct Leadership Lesson for Each Week of the Year*

53. Lincoln's First Rule of Leadership

As soon as you start reading the e-mail, your blood starts to boil. You are being accused, criticized, or demeaned. Your face turns red. Your body tenses. You can't wait to reply. Fingers sledgehammer the keyboard. Setting the record straight becomes your singular focus. Each word scrolling on screen brings vindication. Finally, you hit the send button and waves of satisfaction wash over you.

In the scenario above, you have just succumbed to an emotional hijacking or amygdala hijacking as coined by Daniel Goleman when referring to the part of the brain that processes feelings. No one likes to be criticized. In fact, our bodies respond to criticism and mistruths by sending more cortisol to our brain. This chemical shuts down the reasoning center of our brains and activates the protection center, causing us to perceive greater negativity than actually exists. This stirs the fight or flight reaction that is part of our instinctive behavior.[339]

Emotional hijacking is the opposite of emotional intelligence, which is built upon recognizing, understanding, and managing yours as well as your followers' emotions while also utilizing this capability to motivate. If you cannot regulate your own emotions, how are you going to understand and empathize with your followers? If criticism enrages you, how will you ever be able to lead your followers effectively? Shouldn't leaders' motivation originate with the idea of continually growing as a leader instead of disproving the doubts of others?

President Lincoln understood these things. When he perceived criticism, Lincoln followed a self-imposed rule. Just like you, he allowed himself to be emotionally hijacked. Lincoln quickly authored an angry rebuttal, but instead of depositing the letter in the mail, he placed the letter in his jacket pocket. Approximately twenty-four hours after doing so, President Lincoln retrieved the letter and reread it. Many times, the letter ended up in the garbage with Lincoln understanding how his emotions had compromised his ability to reasonably assess what was being said about him. As much as he hated to admit it, people made

---

[339] J. Glaser, *Conversational Intelligence: How Great Leaders Build Trust and Get Extraordinary Results*, Bibliomotion, Inc., (2014).

valid points, and when addressed, these criticisms helped Lincoln to improve as a leader.

The next time you receive criticism, fight the urge to strike back. Resist the effects of cortisol overload. Look deep within yourself and ask if the critique represents an opportunity to improve. Have you ever hit the send button and wished you hadn't?

54. Lincoln's Second Rule of Leadership

When you direct a follower to do something and the follower

chooses to ignore said direction, how do you feel as the leader? Are you

disappointed or angry? What if this same follower ignored your

direction a second time? Would your reaction change? Would you be

angrier? What if you went to question this follower and the follower

deliberately dismissed you? Would you be upset? Are you inclined to

discipline this person? President Lincoln was, but when presented with

this situation, he did things and reacted in ways most of us would not

expect.

On November 13, 1861, President Lincoln traveled to General

George McClellan's home accompanied by his Secretary of State, John

Seward, and his presidential secretary, John Hay. When they arrived,

McClellan was out, so they waited inside McClellan's home. McClellan

returned home shortly after Lincoln had arrived, but instead of greeting

Lincoln, McClellan chose to ignore Lincoln and went straight to bed.

Further, McClellan instructed his porter to wait for thirty minutes before

advising President Lincoln of his declination to meet with the group.

Upon leaving, Hay was extremely upset and inquired if the President felt

the same way. Lincoln calmly responded by saying, "Better at this time not to be making points of etiquette and personal dignity."[340]

At the time of the personal indignation, Lincoln still believed McClellan to be the best general to lead the Union forces. Although Lincoln intentionally never returned to McClellan's home, he did not let personal judgment get in the way of a practical decision, so Lincoln allowed McClellan to retain his position. Eventually Lincoln lost confidence in McClellan, and in March 1962, McClellan was relieved of his duties.

As soon as McClellan was disciplined, Lincoln instructed one of his advisors to immediately visit McClellan. The advisor was surprised by Lincoln's directive. When the advisor inquired as to the purpose of the McClellan visit, Lincoln stressed the importance of rebuilding McClellan's personal confidence. The directive surprised the advisor, inasmuch as President Lincoln had just fired McClellan. Lincoln, sensing the confusion, explained his directive by telling the advisor that General McClellan, even though he failed in this moment, still had skills that could prove useful to the Union in the future. President Lincoln wanted McClellan to be ready if it was necessary to utilize his skills.

---

[340] Accessed July 6, 2015, http://www.history.com/this-day-in-history/mcclellan-snubs-lincoln.

How many of us could have ignored the personal slights and the open insubordination? How many of us would have felt a compelling urge to prove to McClellan who was the boss? How many of us would have written McClellan off forever? How many of us, consciously or unconsciously, put our needs ahead of our followers?

President Lincoln was able to set aside personal feelings and recognize value in people regardless of how they felt about him or chose to treat him. To Lincoln, the Union's preservation was his first and foremost priority. As we evaluate our ourselves, do we allow our needs to take priority or do we take the view of Lincoln and try to find value in people even when they don't necessarily deserve it?

55. When President Kennedy Fell Victim to Groupthink

Have you ever been a leader of a team that jelled perfectly? Did each team member have skills that complemented the others'? Did it seem like everybody was reading from the same page? As the leader, were you happy when the group continued to come to agreement on ideas and solutions? Are you aware that if this has happened to you as a group member or as a leader, you may be more inclined to fall victim to a phenomenon known as groupthink?

"Groupthink" is the term used to describe the instance where members of a group are so agreeable and embedded into the team dynamic they overlook the possibility that their solution to a problem could be totally wrong. In these instances, group members often look only at the evidence supporting their decision, thereby inflicting confirmation bias in their decision-making process. Even if someone in the group recognized that something was wrong with the project, they would be reluctant to offer the contrary evidence fearing it would disrupt the group's harmony.

In 1986, the National Aeronautics and Space Administration (NASA) launched the space shuttle *Challenger* on a cold Florida day, six days after the intended launch date. Seventy-three seconds into the flight, the spacecraft exploded. Subsequent investigation revealed that groupthink played a major role in the tragic event. It seems that engineers had warned NASA leaders about a potential problem with a part called an O-ring. In testing, the O-ring didn't perform as expected when the temperature was below a certain temperature. On the day of the launch, the outside temperature was significantly lower than the calibrated acceptable temperature level.

At the time of the launch, NASA was under great pressure to get the space shuttle back into space. Engineers and their NASA counterparts had discussions about the O-ring on the day of launch. Despite these discussions, the group, however, bent to the pressure of groupthink when the launch director got the chief engineer to advise that he could not guarantee the O-Ring would fail if the launch took place in the cold temperature. The group, hearing what they wanted to hear, then approved the launch despite managerial safeguards intended to keep the launch from happening. The O-rings eventually failed after launch, causing seven crewmembers to die, including Christa McAuliffe, who was supposed to be the first teacher in space.

The NASA launch team certainly did not intend for the tragic event

to occur. Rather, they fell victim to the belief that launching the shuttle

was appropriate despite clear evidence the launch should have been

delayed. The team fell prey to collective rationalization discrediting and

explaining away the potential dangers. This is a classic symptom of

groupthink.[341]

Even prior to the space shuttle *Challenger*, President Kennedy and

his advisors also fell victim to groupthink. When President Kennedy

realized what happened, he took an important step to ensure

groupthink would not happen again. President Kennedy approached his

brother, Robert, and gave specific instructions on what Robert was to

do to ensure President Kennedy did not fall victim to groupthink again.

Whenever the President took a position, Robert Kennedy was to take

the opposite position—even in cases where he agreed with the

President. By doing so, President Kennedy ensured he at least heard and

considered a contrary argument to what was being proposed.

A conflicting point of view is normally the last thing a cohesive

---

[341] I. L. Janis and L. Mann, *Decision-Making: A Psychological Analysis of Conflict, Choice, and Commitment* (New York: Free Press, 1977).

group wants to consider. As history has shown us, however, that dissenting voice can be the difference between making a good decision and a bad decision. As a leader, can you afford to fall victim to groupthink? The next time someone questions you or your group's decisions, instead of asking "why", maybe we should be asking "why not."

About the Author

In 2011, Michael "Bret" Hood was chosen to be part of a select team dedicated to developing new executive leadership development programs for the FBI. Drawing on his twenty-five years of experience as a special agent, supervisor, and leader in the FBI, Bret took new and unique approaches to designing, developing, and implementing completely interactive instructional blocks designed to leverage the personal experiences of participants to drive learning. For his efforts, Bret received FBI Director awards for innovation and knowledge.

Bret has served as an adjunct professor of leadership for the University of Virginia, teaching leadership and ethics course at both the undergraduate and graduate level. As an advanced master instructor and facilitator for the FBI, Bret created ten-week innovative and completely interactive programs to further the leadership development of domestic and international law-enforcement executives who attended the prestigious FBI National Academy. To date, Bret has also led approximately fifty US delegations to foreign countries to instruct and share knowledge with our foreign law-enforcement counterparts. This book is designed to provide an experience similar to Bret's leadership classes, with the goal being to provoke thought, question perceptions and perspectives, engage in deep self-assessment, and most of all...to have fun. Bret continues to travel the world, training public and private-sector entities on leadership as well as financial crime and other topics through his website, www.21puzzles.com. Bret's e-mail is 21puzzles@gmail.com.

Made in the USA
Columbia, SC
04 July 2018